LiveWork&Play in
AUSTRALIA

*A working holiday and gap year guide
for overseas visitors
for our New Zealand neighbours
and Australian residents of all ages*

LiveWork&Play in

AUSTRALIA

*A working holiday and gap year guide
for overseas visitors
for our New Zealand neighbours
and Australian residents of all ages*

Sharyn McCullum

LiveWork&Play in Australia

Published by
LiveWork&Play Publications
PO Box 155
Camberwell VIC 3124, Australia

www.liveworkplay.com

Email: sharyn@liveworkplay.com

National Library of Australia Cataloguing-in-Publication entry
Author:	McCullum, Sharyn.
Title:	Live Work & Play in Australia: the ultimate working holiday guide / Sharyn McCullum
Edition:	2nd ed.
ISBN:	9780980532401 (pbk.)
Subjects:	Employment agencies--Australia--Directories.
	Australia--Guidebooks
Dewey Number:	919.4

The author and publisher have attempted to ensure the information is the latest available at the time of going to press. Neither the author nor the publisher is responsible for changes which may occur.

Any organisations mentioned are listed in alphabetical order. Their listing goes not constitute recommendation by the author or publisher.

The author and publisher cannot take responsibility for any losses incurred by transactions on the Internet. It is up to the individual to confirm the website is secure and free of viruses before sending or receiving details.

CONTENTS

Aboriginal Australia; ANZAC Day; Aussie tucker; barbecues; blue/bluey; beach; bushfires; bushrangers; clothes; currency; cyclones; dates; deadliest creatures; departure tax; disabilty awareness; drinking; driving; eating out; eucalyptus oil; emergency numbers; fauna; gay and lesbian scene; GST; heat and humidity; lingo; metric system; Ozzie stereotypes; politics/government; post; public holidays; religions; shopping; skin cancer; social events for the calendar; sporting mad; time zones; tipping; Tourist Refund Scheme; TV; World Heritage-listed areas

Part II – Living in Australia

Part III – Working in Australia

Part IV – Playing in Australia

Introduction

G'day and welcome to *LiveWork&Play in Australia* – the ultimate working holiday and gap year guide for overseas visitors, students, our New Zealand neighbours and Australian residents of all ages.

The first things that come to most minds whenever Australia is mentioned are kangaroos, beaches, red outback landscapes and aborigines. Australia is often perceived as a very desirable holiday destination but also a very remote one. This is why an extended holiday spent living, working and playing in Australia will help you truly appreciate the landscape and the people that inhabit its shores.

If you are reading this you are obviously contemplating spending time living, working and playing in Australia. Whether it be lazing on a beach in the Whitsunday Islands or anywhere along the coastline, exploring the outback and learning about our indigenous culture or working hard in a major city or country area, this guide has something to offer.

You don't have to be a gregarious child of adventure to enjoy Australia. All you need is to be a resident or have a passport, a visa, a desire to experience the culture and the countryside, the will to take any work available and a penchant for a good time – well, that's my theory anyway!

Unfortunately many overseas visitors arrive in Australia and find themselves with no friends, family, work, accommodation and wonder: What do I do now? Similarly, many Australians can feel this way. However, hopefully this won't happen to you because with a little pre-planning and knowledge of available opportunities any worries should be minimal.

It is up to you how and where you spend your time in Australia. The role of this travel guide is to suggest useful information to assist you in living, working and playing here. The book is divided into four sections.

Part I is the Essential Stuff and is written to help you get started so you can hit the ground running. It covers the information you need to know and do like passports, visas, when to travel, insurance, packing, gay and lesbian travel, discount cards, ways to travel to Australia, how much money to bring and the best ways to bring it, etc.

Part II is the Living section. It covers short and long-term accommodation options available plus has many useful contacts for finding somewhere to unpack.

Part III is the Working section, that unfortunate part of our working holiday that we must do so as to fund our travels. This section is divided into two parts, Working in Australia and the A-Z of Jobs. The Working part talks about how to find work through newspapers, websites, recruitment agencies, etc. while the A-Z of Jobs offers an extensive listing of employment available including bar work, hospitality, busking, accounting, jackaroo/jillaro, secretarial, labouring, picking fruit and vegetables, volunteering, etc. along with employment contact details for landing jobs.

Part IV is my favourite part and is the Playing section. This section covers the various travel options for travelling around Australia like car pooling, coach, train, cycling and plane and also has an extensive section on suggestions of things to see and do including the popular routes travellers travel. These include traversing the East Coast, travelling up/down the middle, across the bottom and over the top.

Whatever is motivating you to live, work and play in Australia, read on and enjoy your time.

Sharyn McCullum

PART 1 – Essential Stuff

As stated in the Introduction, this book is written for anyone who wants to live, work and play in Australia and that includes Australian residents, our New Zealand neighbours and overseas travellers.

As someone arriving in Australia as a working holiday maker needs to organise themselves differently to an Australian resident about to travel in their own country, you will all find information pertinent to your own case to help you get organised.

This chapter has been set out with major headings with appropriate information underneath. This should make it easier for you to find the information you are looking for. Please read the sections you feel pertinent to your own case. Even skim over the other sections you may not think are relevant because you just might find something of interest. So come on, let's get ready, set and go to live, work and play in Australia.

Can you go? – Passport & visas

Before you can live, work and play in Australia you must confirm that you are entitled to do so. Australian citizens, of course, do not require a visa to work in their own country, but citizens from other countries do.

There are a number of visas available. These include visas for just a holiday, for working holidays, to emigrate and to study. There are also special conditions for New Zealand citizens. Whatever category visa you are hoping to apply for and enter Australia under, please refer to the appropriate section following.

Passport

Non-Australian citizens will need a fully valid passport to enter Australia. If you don't have one, you had better get yourself one. You will not be allowed to enter Australia without one.

A passport is an essential item when travelling abroad. It authenticates your identity and is required so you can enter and leave other countries in the world. You may also need it if stopped in a foreign country and asked to prove your identity.

Most passports issued are valid for 10 years. If you already have one, check the expiry date. It is essential that your passport does not expire within six months of entering Australia. If it does, you had better get yourself a new one.

Visas

Everyone who comes to Australia must have a visa.

A visa is an endorsement stamped in your passport by a foreign government and grants permission for you to enter other countries. Originally the term comes from the Latin word for 'see' and basically means the officials of the country have seen your passport and decided it is alright for you to enter their country. However, a visa stamped in your passport is only a recommendation allowing you in, you still need to arrive and gain clearance from Immigration officials at a port of entry.

Australia has a number of visas available to overseas travellers and these include:

Visitor/Tourist Visa

If you are planning a visit to Australia of up to three months you can apply for the Visitor/Tourist visa. You must note that this visa does NOT allow you to undertake any work whatsoever while in Australia.

Australia has an Electronic Travel Authority (ETA) system. The ETA is an electronically stored authority for travel to Australia. It replaces the visa label or stamp in your passport. When you arrive in Australia your details are called up by a Custom's Officer on their computer system and voila, there are your details. ETAs are issued in around 10 seconds of being requested. Today nationals of 29 countries are eligible to apply for an ETA that is available through travel agents in North America, UK and Western Europe and in some countries in South East Asia.

If you apply for an ETA and plan on staying in Australia for a maximum of three months, there is no visa fee. However, staying longer than three months incurs a A$45 processing fee.

Full details regarding the visitor/tourist visa should be obtained from your nearest Australian High Commission, Consulate or on the Department of Immigration website www.immi.gov.au.

Working Holiday Visa

Australia's Immigration Department's website advises that "The Working Holiday Program aims to promote international understanding, through helping young people experience the culture of another country. It provides opportunities for resourceful, self-reliant and adaptable young people to holiday in Australia and to supplement their funds through incidental employment".

Since its inception working holiday maker numbers have been increasing, with the most coming from the United Kingdom, The Republic of Ireland, Japan, Germany, Canada and The Netherlands.

Australia currently has reciprocal working holiday arrangements with: Belgium; Canada; Cyprus, Republic of; Denmark; Estonia; Finland; France; Germany; HKSAR the Hong Kong Special Administrative Region (HKSAR) of the People's Republic of China; Ireland, Republic of; Italy; Japan; Korea, Republic of; Malta; The Netherlands; Norway; Sweden; Taiwan; United Kingdom.

Therefore, if you hold a passport from one of these countries, are aged between 18-30 years of age inclusive and do not have any dependents, you will be allowed to apply for the working holiday visa. If successful, the visa will allow you to enter and stay in Australia to live, work and play for 12 months. However, if you work in 'specified work' for at least three months you may qualify for another 12 months working holiday visa giving you a total of 24 months in Australia. Specified work includes fruit and vegetable picking, mining, construction, animal cultivation, tree farming and felling, fishing and pearling or work undertaken as a volunteer or through the Willing Workers on Organic Farms (WWOOF) scheme. Specified work must be undertaken in a specified eligible regional Australian postcode area. A list of eligible postcode areas is listed at http://www.immi.gov.au/visitors/working-holiday/417/postcodes.htm.

Full details regarding the Working Holiday Visa should be obtained from your nearest Australian High Commission, Consulate or on the Department of Immigration website www.immi.gov.au

Work and Holiday Visa

The Work and Holiday Visa is for tertiary educated people aged 18 to 30 who want to travel and work for up to 12 months in Australia. This visa allows you to supplement the cost of your holiday through periods of temporary or casual employment. Most countries under this visa program have a limit on the number of Work and Holiday Visas issued per year.

Currently, the Work and Holiday Visa arrangement is in place for people from Chile, Thailand, Turkey and the United States of America. Australia has signed Work and Holiday Visa arrangements with Bangladesh, Malaysia and Indonesia which need formalising. Please check with the Department of Immigration to their progress.

You can apply for a Work and Holiday Visa if you:
- are aged 18 to 30 years (inclusive) on the date you apply
- hold a passport from a country that has a Work and Holiday arrangement with Australia
- have a letter of support from your government (not required by applicants from the USA)
- are not accompanied by dependent children
- have not previously entered Australia on a Working Holiday (417) or Work and Holiday (462) visa.

Visit www.immi.gov.au for the latest details.

Student Visa

Overseas students who wish to undertake study in a registered course in Australia may apply for a student visa. Current student visas available include:

English Language Intensive Courses for Overseas Students (ELICOS)
Applies to stand-alone English language courses that lead to a certificate I, II, III or IV, or that result in no formal Australian award.

Primary or secondary school course
Applies to primary, junior secondary or senior secondary school courses, and approved secondary school exchange programs.

Vocational education and training
Applies to Certificates I, II, III or IV (except ELICOS), diploma, advanced diploma, vocational graduate certificate or vocational graduate diploma courses.

Higher education
Applies to a Bachelor degree, associate degree, graduate certificate, graduate diploma, or Masters by coursework.

Postgraduate research
Applies to Masters by research or a doctoral degree.

Non-award
Applies to non-award foundation studies, or other full-time courses or components of courses not leading to an Australian award.

AusAID and Defence
Applies to students sponsored by AusAID or the Australian Department of Defence undertaking full-time courses of any type.

Student Guardians
Parents or relatives can apply for a visa to stay in Australia as the guardian of a student who is studying in Australia.

Full details regarding any of the student visas should be obtained from your nearest Australian High Commission, Consulate or at Australia's Department of Immigration website at www.immi.gov.au.

New Zealand passport holders

For more than 90 years Australia has allowed New Zealand citizens to come and live and work here. In 1973 the Trans Tasman Travel Arrangement was introduced. This allows Australian and New Zealand citizens to move between, and to live, work and play freely in either country without restrictions and without the need to apply for authority to enter the other country.

All New Zealanders will need a passport to travel to Australia. On arrival you will receive a 'special category visa' (SCV) which will allow you to live, work and play as long as you wish.

On 26 February 2001 both the New Zealand and Australian governments announced new social security arrangements between the two countries. Basically, the changes affect those who have lived in both countries. It will change the way some benefits and pensions are paid, and affect eligibility for some other benefits.

New Zealanders wishing to live, work and play in Australia may wish to obtain more details from the New Zealand Ministry of Foreign Affairs and Trade www.mft.govt.nz or call the Australian Consulate General in Auckland on Tel: (09) 303 2429. Details can also be obtained at Australia's Department of Immigration website at www.immi.gov.au.

Work and Travel Programs/Organisations

Many working holiday makers head to Australia independently. However, if you have never travelled before, or are travelling solo and are feeling a little nervous, you may be interested in a work and travel program. These programs offer a number of services including arranging your air ticket, insurance, orientation before and after your arrival, accommodation for your first few nights, employment assistance and support during your stay. Some provide group travel which means you will meet other like-minded

travellers. They can even pre-arrange a bank account, mail forwarding, phone card, Email access, apply for your Tax File Number
and arrange an airport pick-up for you. Having all of these things
available to you obviously gives you (and your parents) a reassur-
ing and secure feeling. It must be noted that you need to qualify
for the working holiday visa or work and holiday visa to be accepted on to programs.

Programs are available if you are coming from Canada, Germany, Ireland, Japan, the Netherlands, the United Kingdom and
the United States. Companies include:

Coming from Canada:
The Canadian Federation of Students (CFS) runs
SWAP Australia www.swap.ca
Email: swapinfo@swap.ca

Coming from Germany:
Step In GmbH www.step-in.de
Tel: (0228) 956 95-00
Email: info@step-in.de

Coming from Ireland:
USIT Travel www.usit.ie
Tel: (01) 602 1906

Coming from Japan:
Council Exchanges www.cieej.or.jp

Coming from the United Kingdom:
BUNAC (www.bunac.org.uk) in conjunction with
International Exchange Programs (www.iep.org.au)
Council Exchanges UK www.councilexchanges.org.uk.

Coming from the United States:
BUNAC www.bunac.org

Australian companies include:
IEP (International Exchange Program) www.iep.org.au
1300 300 912 (for the cost of a local call)
Email: info@iep.org.au
Melbourne office: Level 3, 362 La Trobe St
Tel: (03) 9329 3866
Sydney office: Level 18, 233 Castlereagh St
Tel: (02) 9299 0399

Work & Travel Company
234 Sussex St, Sydney NSW 2000
Tel: (02) 8987 3700
Email: info@worktravelcompany.com.au

Migration agents

If your visa application is rejected, or you do not qualify for any of the visas, you may wish to contact a specialist migration agent. If you wish to contact such an agent, you should ensure they are a registered agent. In Australia agents must be registered with the Migration Agents Registration Authority (MARA). For more details about MARA and to view its online database, visit www.themara.com.au.

When to go

Some people can throw caution to the wind and jump on a plane or in a car and travel to or in Australia without hesitation, while others plan every minute detail months in advance. The influencing factors in deciding when to go travelling to and around Australia include your bank balance, the weather, the cost of airfares and accommodation, the availability of work opportunities and the possibility of attending special events.

Bank balance

For those of you arriving from overseas on a working holiday visa it is stipulated when you apply for the visa you need at least A$4500 in your bank account. This is so you can support yourself during the early days of your stay.

No matter who you are, working holiday maker or Australian resident about to travel your own country you will definitely need money to be able to enjoy Australia to its full extent. You don't want to miss out on something just because you don't have enough money! So the more you can save before your trip the better. But how much? Everyone is different on where they want to stay, what they eat and what they want to see. But budget for the following:

Accommodation, per night	$..............
Food, x 3 meals	$..............
Entertainment,	$.............
Transport,	$..............
Souvenirs	$..............

The weather and prime times to travel

Someone once said to me "I come from a country that has some of the coldest winters in the world – if I can follow the sun and avoid a winter, then I'm gunna."

It is possible to have a year-round summer if that's what you want. Simply stay in the southern states during the summer months (December, January, February) then head north during the winter months (June, July, August). So when to arrive in or begin travelling Australia? Any time really. As for travelling the country, there are prime times for seeing some areas. For instance, the outback and the Great Barrier Reef are far better during the winter months as the weather is far more stable than the summer months that bring tropical storms and cyclones.

Unlike most Northern Hemisphere countries where the further north you travel the colder it becomes, Australia is the opposite. The further north you travel the hotter it becomes. During the summer months (remember the seasons in the Southern Hemisphere are opposite to those in the Northern Hemisphere) the weather can be very uncomfortable for the traveller who is not used to it.

A big influence on the northern half of Australia is the Tropic of Capricorn, which runs through it. This gives the top half two seasons: wet and dry. During the wet season (November to April) days are hot and humid with a lot of rain and usually a cyclone or two around the coast. The stingers (jellyfish) are also out in force in the ocean.

You can still visit the area during this time, after all many Australians live there, but you will encounter more rain and hotter days with high humidity, which many travellers find uncomfortable. If your plan is to laze on a beach in Queensland during this time you may be a little disappointed. Or if you want to experience the outback you might find it too excruciatingly hot to enjoy with temperatures in the high 30s (celcius) 90s (Fahrenheit).

During the winter months in the north the weather is more pleasant. There is less rain if you want to lie on a beach, and outback days are warm and dry with cool evenings. Not many people realise that the desert areas become cool during the dry winter season as the desert is like a cold-blooded animal; it doesn't retain its heat when the sun goes down.

The bottom half of the country – New South Wales, Victoria, Tasmania, South Australia and the bottom half of Western Australia – have four quite distinct seasons. It can be very cold during winter with snow appearing in the mountains and during summer there are long hot days. Cool changes are often prayed for to lower the temperature. Many a day is spent on the coastline lapping up the sun.

If you want to see the sights in prime times, stay south during the summer months then head north for winter. Remember though that many travellers travel during prime time, and accommodation can be harder to come by and more expensive.

Airfares and accommodation

Airfares

If travelling from overseas to Australia, the cost of your airfare will be high on the priority list as this cost can influence when to go. There are high, low and shoulder season airfares. Of course, airfares are most expensive during the high season.

The high season is December to February (Oz summer time). The low season is April to August, which is the end of autumn and all of winter, while the shoulder seasons are autumn and spring. The difference in price from high to low can be a few hundred dollars. In traveller terms, this can mean a couple of weeks' hostel accommodation. The high season can begin at any time in December and end at any time in February, so check with your travel agent.

Some prefer to leave as close as possible to the end of the low season to take advantage of a cheaper airfare, but arrive at the beginning of the next season. If you are going to travel during the low season, book early, as many people – especially those who have just read this – could be looking to do so as well.

Also, book early if you are looking to arrive in December, as you will be vying for bum-space with many Australians returning home for Christmas after their jaunts around the world.

There isn't a seasonal influence on domestic airfares. The airlines servicing Australia offer some very reasonably priced airfares. There are more details on air travel in our Travelling Options section in our Playing chapter.

Accommodation

Prices for short-term accommodation (camping, motels, holiday flats, etc.) increase and sometimes double during school holidays, especially over Christmas and New Year when many Australians take their holidays. Hostel prices usually remain constant (although some places can increase their rates during holiday periods). You may need to book in advance during the busy times to ensure you secure a bed/room.

Work opportunities

Just as the weather can influence your travel plans, so might the availability of work opportunities. Under the various headings in the A-Z of Jobs section, I have tried to indicate the busy and quiet times. Working holiday makers heading to Sydney for the Christmas and New Year period (which many do to attend Christmas Day celebrations on Bondi Beach), should try to be there around November. This is because you're not only vying for positions with other backpackers, but with university students who have a three-month summer vacation and with school students who have a six-week summer break.

Overall, work is available year-round although some positions, like hospitality work, can be influenced by the seasons. Most offices close over the Christmas and New Year period or have a skeleton staff. Building and trade work also shuts down over this period from two to four weeks.

Particular events

The timing of a particular event you wish to see or participate in may influence your decision on when to go or when to travel; for instance: would you like to go whale watching in Hervey Bay? Would you like to see a cricket match or a game of one of the football codes? Would you like to see the Sydney Harbour Bridge lit up with fireworks on New Year's Eve? Do you want to go to the Gay and Lesbian Mardi Gras? Would you like to attend the Melbourne Cup, which stops the nation for three minutes every year? Would you like to night dive Western Australia's Ningaloo Reef during the one-night-a-year when the coral spawn? (See Useful Information for a listing of major events.) If there is something you particularly want to see or participate in you should try and see or do it – because you don't know when you will be back! Is a saving of A$200 worth it, if you miss out on something you really want to see?

How to get to Australia

As a number of oceans and seas surround Australia, there are really only two ways to reach its distant shores. Boat (which can take several weeks or months) and, of course, the most popular and quickest method, plane.

Ocean cruising isn't as popular these days as it once was but many ocean vessels still visit Australia's shores. You could arrive as a freighter passenger or crew, on an ocean liner as a passenger or crew, or perhaps as crew on a private yacht.

There are many airlines flying into Australia, which means Australia can be part of a world tour or can be visited on its own.

Depending on the route chosen, your flight can take a few ice-filled drinks, wrestles with packets of peanuts, a dinner, a light refreshment, breakfast, hopefully a snooze, a couple of trips to the loo and a movie or two. But how many hours? Well, from the UK and Europe anywhere between 24 to 36 hours. From North America anywhere between 14 to 25 hours. From Japan about 12 hours. From New Zealand about two to three hours. From Africa, Asia and South America anywhere between 10 to 15 hours.

Many like to break the long trip with a stop-over, which those who suffer from sinus problems might appreciate, as exposure to long periods of cabin air can cause the nose to become dried out and stuffy. People who wear contact lenses might want to wear glasses for a long flight as the cabin air can dry your eyes. A stop-over might also help alleviate jetlag and any other effects associated with flying, like swollen ankles and Deep Vein Thrombosis. For more information, refer to our Travelling Well section in our Travel options chapter.

Smokers might also like a stop-over as airlines flying to Australia are non-smoking.

There are different tickets available which are valid for a year, such as a round-the-world ticket, although if you are hoping to spend a full year in Australia this ticket might not be the one for you. You might want to enquire about 'open jaw' tickets where you can fly into one city and out of another.

Australia's international gateways are Sydney, Melbourne, Brisbane, Darwin, Cairns, Perth and Adelaide. Therefore you could fly into Perth, travel overland to Sydney for a flight out, or fly into Sydney and out of Darwin or Cairns. The choice is yours.

The most popular arrival destination is Sydney. If you plan to arrive there, you might wish to request a window seat on the left side of the plane. This is because most planes approach the airport from a northerly direction, which means you will fly in over the city and receive a superb bird's-eye view of the Harbour Bridge and the Opera House. If your seat is on the right side don't worry, as you will see the sprawling metropolis of Sydney reaching the Great Dividing Range in the distance.

Although we all like a bargain, remember that cheap flights aren't always the best. Sometimes there are restrictions; there might be five stop-overs before arrival in Australia, or they only arrive once or twice a week, which means you will have to fit in your plans around them. If you don't mind, then go with that airline but do shop around to find a ticket that suits you.

There are many possibilities, so haunt travel agents, watch out for specials listed in papers and surf the Internet for specialist travel sites until you find something that suits you, your aspirations and your budget.

Packing

Packing is an arduous task at the best of times; trying to squeeze in everything you think you'll need for your travels in Australia can be horrendous.

There could be some of you who imagine that all you'll need to pack is swim wear, a towel for the beach, a pair of shorts and walking shoes for the outback. For those following the sun this might be all you need, but weather can change and Australia does have cold weather.

Before you begin to pack ask yourself, what kind of travelling will you be doing? For how long? Once you've answered these questions you will be able to choose the type of luggage that suits you. No matter what kind of travel you will be doing, you will want your luggage to be easily manoeuvred in and out of your transport, and easy to carry around. A backpack is easier to carry around than a suitcase, especially if you happen to be walking in the red dirt of the outback. However, if you are having a two-week vacation staying in the one place and lying on the beach all day and partying at night, a suitcase with wheels will be just fine.

There are various backpack designs available so spend some time seeing what they offer. Some are top opening, while others have zippers. I prefer packs with zippers as I've seen people with top-opening ones having to dig deep, or unpack their other belongings, to find what they are looking for. Those with zippers can also be locked. Try backpacks on and get the right size for your back length. If you decide to stick with a suitcase, invest in a trolley or a suitcase with wheels and telescopic handle.

You will also need a small daypack or carry bag to hold your camera, MP3 player, mobile phone, etc. This could also double as luggage for overnight or weekend trips, so take that into consideration when choosing. Some backpacks come with a zip-off daypack and removable toiletries bag. Don't forget to label your luggage inside and out and keep it locked. Make it stand out by tying ribbon on it, so you'll recognise it on sight.

Once you have your luggage, you can consider what to pack. Ask yourself these questions before you do: How can I avoid looking like a tourist? Am I travelling to other countries before I arrive in Australia? Will these countries have dress regulations? When am I arriving or travelling in Australia – summer or winter? What type of work am I looking for?

OK, so how not to look like a tourist. Being a tourist can attract professional thieves, so try and blend in. It is hard not to be seen at some stage with your luggage, but try and find a place to store it as soon as possible.

I have heard people say: 'I dress down because people seem to leave me alone that way.' I have found this comment true in my travels and you too can take this into consideration when packing. Don't dress like you have loads of money and don't wear the family jewels (unless you're off to a ball or the races) or you'll stand out from the casually dressed Australians.

Australians like to advertise where they have been on their travels or where they are from, so try to wear T-shirts stating where you've been yourself and where you're from. Other popular T-shirts to wear include those with surf brand names on them and sporting teams. If you blend in, some tourist just might ask you for directions!

Australia doesn't have any religious restrictions influencing dress, but if you are travelling to other countries before or after your Australian visit find out whether these countries have dress regulations.

You will need to pack for all types of weather in Australia. You will need swimwear, shorts and T-shirts for the warm weather. Loose-fitting clothes are best in hot weather and it's possible you will make a few changes during the day. When it gets cold, especially in the southern states, you will need winter woollies and possibly an overcoat.

For work you will need suitable clothes. Under each work opportunity I have tried to include the clothes you are required to wear and any utensils you are expected to have.

You might need a jumper or cardigan for indoors during summer, which probably sounds ridiculous to you now, but the hotter it is outside, the colder it can be indoors. Sometimes it can be too cold. But there is nothing like that 'Ahhhh' sensation you'll feel when you walk through the automatic doors to a gush of tingling coolness after being in the heat.

Going away usually means you want to buy new things to take with you. This can deplete your savings for your trip. When travelling, old clothes are just as useful and often preferable. Sometimes on a two or three day camping trip you might spend days in the same clothes, and in the outback the red dirt can get into everything – permanently.

The travelling backpackers' uniform is shorts, T-shirt and sandals during the day, and for going out, jeans and a T-shirt or a loose-fitting dress, and shoes.

For compact travel items and knick-knacks, look in disposal and camping stores, bric-a-brac stores, travel agents, bag shops, specialist outdoor stores and YHA travel shops.

All the following suggestions are just that; suggestions. Makeshift, already acquired, or borrowed items will do the job just as effectively as new items. A lot of things can be bought in Australia when you need them, so even though it's nice to have new things to take away, save your money for your travels.

Suggested list of items

Underwear Maybe enough for a week or two, as you don't know when you'll be able to wash it while travelling, but it's up to you. Maybe you want to hang free and loose. Cotton garments that breathe in the heat are highly recommended.

Swimwear Guys usually wear Speedos or board shorts. Girls wear bikinis and one-piece suits. You may wish to have a couple of pairs if you are planning to spend a lot of time in the sun – after all, you don't want to be seen in the same swimwear day after day! Swimwear can usually be bought all year round, especially in the northern states.

T-shirts A couple should do you – one off and one on – although in really hot weather you might make a couple of changes during the day.

Shorts One or two casual pairs to wear to the beach and for sightseeing, plus a good pair for going out. Yes – during hot summer nights dressy shorts are worn out.

Hat With a wide brim to keep the sun off the back of your neck and face. Baseball caps are also popular.

Sunglasses It is advisable to wear these at all times when outside, as a lot of eye diseases are related to over exposure to ultraviolet rays. Try to get a pair that also protects the side of your eyes.

Sunscreen It is advised to wear SPF15+ or SPF30+ unless you're after the "lobster" look. Bottles/tubes can be bought easily in chemists, supermarkets and shops near beaches. Try and wear moisturisers with sun block already in them for added protection.

After-sun cream

Towel/s One that doubles as a beach towel and a shower towel.

Hand towel Good to take on long journeys when you need to freshen up. It feels much better than paper towel or toilet paper.

Walking shoes/hiking boots/joggers Wear them in before you leave home so you don't get blisters. You might want to spend a little extra for a good quality pair.

Socks A few pairs.

Thongs / Jandals /sandals Very good for wearing to the beach and sightseeing. Some travellers prefer a pair of good soled sandals to walking boots to let their feet breathe. Saves washing socks too. Also good for wearing to the toilet and shower blocks at camp sites and hostels. If it gets cold, you could wear a pair of socks with your sandals.

Leggings/trackpants/sweatpants One or two pairs for cooler weather.

Jeans One or two pairs which can be worn casually or dressed up.

Jumper/sweater/jersey One or two, but try not to bring really bulky ones. You could buy a lamb's wool one in Australia.

Going-out shoes One pair, although if you have dressy sandals these can be worn. During summer, shoes that let your feet breathe are much better to wear than closed-in shoes. If you are sharing a hostel room, non-smelly feet are appreciated.

Going-out outfit One or two.

Work clothes

Coat Can be bulky to carry but will be welcomed in the southern states during winter. A hooded water-proof jacket is preferable.

Gloves Handy for winter. You might need fingerless ones for fruit and vegetable picking during winter.

Snow gear Can easily be rented in the ski fields or in city shops. You will find a lot of surf-and-ski shops – surfing for the summer and skiing for the winter.

Sleeping sheet/bag Very handy for dossing on floors, camping and staying in hostels (though most hostels don't allow sleeping bags nowadays because of strict Australian health regulations).

Hostels will rent out sheets to you if you don't have any and usually supply blankets. On camping trips a sleeping bag will come in
handy, although most tour companies will hire these if you request
it when booking. Sleeping bags vary in quality and the degree of
insulation they provide. When you're camping in the outback during winter (the most pleasant time to go) it can become very cool at
night, reaching single Celsius figures (less than 50°F).

Money belt Apart from being uncomfortable and making one
look like they're pregnant or have a beer gut, these are a safe way
to carry money, travellers' cheques and tickets, etc. Different styles
exist; some you can wear around the neck or shoulder, similar to
a gun holster. Check them out and see what suits you. Or have
compartments sewn into your clothes.

Torch You will be surprised how often one comes in handy.

Travel clothes line and **pegs** It's hard to find a clothes hoist
when you need one. You'll find these handy during your travels,
although camp sites and hostels usually have a launderette with a
washer and a dryer.

Washing powder I've seen small tubes of liquid wash at large
supermarkets and some travel agents. Most hostels/camping
grounds will supply a cup for between 50 cents to A$1.00 via a
machine or from an office attendant.

Plastic bags For dirty washing plus other bits and pieces.
Although plastic bags are being phased out.

MP3 player/iPod

Camera You might wish to purchase this duty-free or buy a
cheap disposable camera, available from chemists and supermarkets. Having a spare **memory stick** for your digital camera will
come in handy.

Travel iron Handy for clothes that need ironing, like work
clothes. You could invest in an iron when you arrive and sell it
when you move on. Many backpackers wear the crumpled look
while travelling. Some laundries have irons available.

Coat hangers A couple are useful if staying put for a while although some accommodation places will supply.

Travel clock You don't want to be late for work now do you? If yours has a loud tick, don't pack it in your luggage as it could be mistaken for a bomb.

Power point adaptor Duty-free shops carry sets of plugs for Australia. Plugs have three prongs so if you are bringing a travel iron, hair dryer or shaver this will be very useful.

Blow-up neck pillow For those long journeys when you might need to sleep sitting up.

Foldaway umbrella For those times you get caught in the rain. It's also useful for taking down to the beach as it protects your skin from the sun.

Passport photos can come in handy.

Needle, thread and scissors Pack these in your checked luggage so you don't set off any metal detector alarms at airports – it's embarrassing. Also, most airline security staff will confiscate small scissors.

Roll-on insect repellent Mosquitoes, flies and other insects are a pain.

Toiletries Bring travel-size, like roll-on deodorant instead of a large can, and two-in-one shampoo and conditioner. Collect the free sachets from magazines. You can always change brands once you've arrived.

Toiletry bag Preferably water-proof for when you take it to the shower.

Sink plug (one size fits all) If you like to shave or wash your face in a basin, as not all hostels or camping grounds provide them in shower blocks.

Toilet roll A very good idea when travelling in the outback and camping. Sometimes the bush is preferable to a public toilet!

CV (curriculum vitae and references) An updated, typed CV and references are essential if you want to obtain work. You could Email yourself a copy or take a USB stick with your CV and scans of important documents. You can also use this to store photos.

Travel diary For all those wonderful memories though many are doing this on-line and uploading their travels to their personal websites.

Address book To keep in contact with old friends and to add new ones take two because this is one of the most commonly lost items. Although many people now use contact function on emails such as Hotmail, Yahoo and gmail – makes for less luggage.

Maps Essential for finding your way around. There are extensive selections available in bookshops, service stations and newsagents. Information centres and hostels will have a free map of the local area. Motoring organisations provide free maps to members.

Writing material

Medicines Brands can differ in Australia. Some medications obtained over-the-counter in some countries may only be available on prescription in Australia. Obtain a supply to cover you for your stay and don't forget to have written permission from your doctor or health department just in case the drug is illegal in Australia or in other countries you will be travelling through.

Multi-vitamins In case you drink too much and don't eat properly.

Condoms A necessity these days.

Constipation/diarrhoea/upset stomach tablets Travelling can do weird things to the digestive system.

Bandaids/plasters

Headache tablets

Sting relief When bitten by insects.

Antiseptic/healing cream For cuts and abrasions.

Travel sickness tablets If you're susceptible to it.

Water purifying tablets/purifier Water is safe to drink in

Australia, although the taste varies from area to area. If it looks suspect, drink bottled water.

Flag Good for flying at sporting events.

OK, you've chosen luggage and gathered everything to take. Now lay it all out on the floor to see what you have. Go get a coffee or tea or your favourite potion then sit in front of your piles and consider why you're taking each item. Convince yourself of its worth or worthlessness. Finally, let's pack.

Everyone has a trick for packing. Some people stack things flat, but one way I find useful for backpacks is rolling clothes up tightly which seems to minimise wrinkles and lets me cram more in. I've also found that packing heavy objects in the middle, close to the back of the pack, will help keep the centre of gravity in the right place.

Keep useful accessories and things you need a lot near the top for easy access. Better still, keep them in your daypack.

Keep in mind any baggage allowances on organised trips and planes (usually 20kg). Airlines have a size and weight limit on cabin luggage so check this out with your travel agent.

To minimise weight, get rid of unnecessary packaging. Take new shirts and pantyhose out of boxes. A friend uses empty spice jars to carry enough toiletries to get to her destination. She also carries money and jewellery in them. I collect the sample sachets of shampoo and conditioner delivered through the post or given away free in magazines. I also request samples at make-up counters.

If travelling on a long-haul flight to Australia and you find you can't fit in everything or are over the 20kg airline allowance and you believe you can't live without all your essentials, you might consider sending luggage as unaccompanied baggage. Ring your airline's cargo department and find out rates and procedures. But try to travel as light as possible it makes life a lot easier. Or budget to buy things during your travels.

Remember to keep something out to wear on the plane, something comfortable, loose fitting and suitable for the weather at your destination. It is suggested you dress nicely when travelling by plane through Asian countries with strict drug regulations, as I have found that people who appear to be scruffy are often singled out to be searched.

You might wish to have some activities to do on the plane: books, music, games, a pack of cards.

The following items are often useful on the plane: an eye mask; socks to keep feet warm; ear plugs to keep out the engine hum; a face towel and toiletries to freshen up; a bottle of spray water to keep face moisturised; a neck rest; sinus tablets.

Money matters

How much to take

'The heaviest baggage for a traveller is an empty purse.' So take as much money as possible.

You will need to budget for expenses such as accommodation, food, sightseeing and spending money.

It is very hard to give you precise cost of many items such as accommodation and food because their costs vary so much from area to area.

How to take it

Open a bank account

A bank account will give you access to your money via banks, ATMs, phone and Internet banking and through EFTPOS (Electronic Funds Transfer at Point of Sale). Overseas visitors may wish to look into whether they can access their current bank account through Australian ATMs. Usually signs such as Maestro means you will have access. Best to check on the charges involved before deciding on this option as the charges can work out to be expensive. Another option for overseas visitors is to open a bank account in Australia from home and transfer funds over. Also if you run out of money, more can easily be sent. Ask your bank if they can do this for you. If they can, request a savings account with an ATM (Automatic Teller Machine) card so that you can use an ATM. For security reasons the card won't be issued until you arrive, but the account can still be used if you go into the bank itself with identification. (See the section Now you've arrived for more information on Australian banks and opening a bank account.) You may also wish to look into Internet banking to access and control your finances at home and abroad.

You ATM card may also be used in supermarkets, shops, restaurants and petrol stations for EFTPOS transactions. You can also ask for cash if your card is accepted.

Credit Card

A credit card will be very useful. The most widely used cards are MasterCard and Visa although other cards are usually accepted. What many travellers do is credit their credit card, pay for goods and services with it, and when they need cash obtain a cash advance. You can obtain cash from ATMs wherever you see machines with the MasterCard and Visa signs, so make sure you have a PIN (Personal Identification Number).

Check the expiry date of your card and make sure it is valid for the entire length of your stay, because you don't want to be caught out. Make sure you take emergency contact numbers in case you lose it. Check with your bank about how to make payments from overseas.

Being able to use EFTPOS and credit cards in this electronic banking world are two methods so much easier than worrying about finding a place to cash travellers' cheques (which aren't that widely used anymore).

Travel money card

Travelex Cash Passport is a prepaid travel money card available in 5 currencies (Euros, Pounds, US, NZ or Australian dollars). A card allows you to withdraw local currency at Visa ATMs with your PIN-protected card. You can reload the card if you use all the available credit. For more details visit www.cashpassport.com.au.

Travellers Cheques

Travellers Cheques were once the most popular way to carry your money overseas. As you've just read there are other preferred options nowadays. Don't dismiss travellers cheques all together now as the beauty of them is that if lost or stolen they can be replaced. They might prove to be a lifesaver if you ever lose or have stolen your credit card and/or ATM card.

Some places charge extortionate commission to cash them for you, especially in the outback. If you do take them, carry denominations of $50 or $100 in Australian dollars, as the commission is usually charged per cheque.

Thomas Cook and American Express travellers' cheques are the most popular and there are offices in Australia able to cash them without charging commission. Other places to exchange them include banks, tourist shops and major hotels. You will most likely have to produce your passport as identification to cash the cheque/s, while having a credit card and/or ATM access will save you having to carry your documents around.

Remember to keep a record of the serial numbers on your travellers' cheques. Stash this list separately from the cheques themselves, and leave a copy at home in case they are lost or stolen.

Sorting your affairs

Add a trusted friend's signature to your bank account

Arrange to pay your bills with a regular electronic transfer, or set up phone banking or Internet banking. You can take the hassle out of managing your money by adding an extra signature to your bank account. Make sure your chosen trusted person accompanies you to your branch to have their signature added to your account and the bank records. This way, the staff will know (or at least one staff member) should know about your situation. This person will then be allowed to operate your account on your behalf. Make sure you leave enough in it so the bills can be paid, and money sent to you if the need arises.

Sign a power of attorney

You can also sign a power of attorney, giving a trusted friend, family member, professional person or body the authority to act on your behalf with regard to your affairs while you are away. The form can be obtained from legal stationers and some newsagents, and the arrangement is valid until revoked.

Make a will

As Katherine Mansfield, a New Zealand author once said: 'Whenever I prepare for a journey I prepare as though for death. Should I never return, all is in order. This is what life has taught me.'

Making a will might be unpleasant and sound absurd to those coming to Australia to visit for a short time, on a working holiday or an Australian travelling their own country but it is a good idea.

You are travelling to enjoy yourself and sometimes you will do things you wouldn't normally do, like bungee jumping, diving a coastal wreck, rock climbing, bush walking, canyoning or learning to surf – each having elements of danger to them that include unforeseen elements such as the weather.

Now I'm not saying the bungee rope will snap, or a shark will be lurking in the wreck, or you'll fall off a cliff or be bitten by a deadly snake in the bush, or be thrown off your surfboard by a whopper wave, but there is nothing worse than leaving your relatives to sort out the legal mess in the wake of your demise. Chances are slim that anything will happen to you, but you never know.

Holiday insurance and medical care

Holiday insurance

Australians, of course, are covered for medical treatment through Medicare and through private health funds. Not many people consider taking out insurance while travelling through their own country. However, depending on the type of travel you will be doing, it may be worth your while to look into some kind of insurance even if it is only to cover cancellation of your trip due to an airline or tour company going broke, lost or stolen cameras or to cover activities such as diving, bungee jumping, white water rafting, etc.

For overseas visitors, holiday insurance is just that; insurance which covers you while you're on holiday so if you are arriving on a working holiday visa make sure you purchase a policy that covers working holidays.

It is wise to shop around and read the fine print on different policies, compare what they cover you for and how much they pay out if things do go wrong.

Trip cancellation, travel documents, medical expenses, luggage and personal effects, accidental death and personal liability are usually covered. Get your travel agent (they will usually refer you to the actual insurer) to go through it with you or make sure you read the fine print.

If you are taking expensive items like a camera, video equipment, laptop, MP3 player, etc. you might wish to take out additional insurance as these aren't usually covered in general policies.

If you think you might participate in activities such as scuba diving, snow or water skiing, bungee jumping, parachuting, paragliding, etc., check if you are covered. If not, you might want to cover yourself for such things. If you find that you have taken out inadequate travel insurance, you can purchase more insurance while in Australia. The specialist backpacker travel agencies can organise this insurance.

Take emergency contact numbers in case something does happen. Should you need to put in a claim make sure you report your loss to someone in authority, like the police, the hotel owner, etc. Obtain a written statement from them to back up your story.

Reciprocal medical arrangements

Australia has reciprocal medical arrangements with the United Kingdom, New Zealand, Sweden, the Netherlands, Finland, Malta, the Republic of Ireland and Italy. If you are from one of these countries, you are covered for medical care in public hospitals in Australia through Medicare. For more details, visit the Health Insurance Commission's website www.hic.gov.au or pop into a Medicare office after you arrive and pick up the brochure 'Visiting Australia'.

Vaccinations

Vaccinations are not required to enter Australia as it is a low-risk country, although it wouldn't hurt (no pun intended) to have childhood shots boosted, plus Hepatitis A, Polio and Tetanus. Have these shots about six weeks ahead of your departure in case you have any adverse reactions.

If you live in a low-risk country, your body has not been exposed to many diseases and you may have a low level of immunity, so if you're travelling through a high-risk country on your way to Australia, you are more susceptible to illnesses. Therefore, check with your doctor or a specialist in travel medicine for the correct vaccinations. Also see if you require a vaccination record as some countries require you to have one before you may enter. Australia does need to see a vaccination record if you are arriving from yellow fever areas (South America and Africa) within six days of being there.

Medical/dental check-up

It is wise to have a check-up with a doctor or dentist before heading off on your travels, as it is horrible being sick while travelling. While at the doctor obtain enough medication to last you for the duration of your travels as, if you are coming from overseas, brands can differ in Australia. As I've said before, some drugs bought over-the-counter in other countries require a prescription in Australia and vice versa. If you do have prescribed drugs on you, carry a note from the prescribing doctor explaining what they are and for whom they have been prescribed.

Private health insurance

There are a number of private health insurance companies in Australia. If you have private health insurance in your own country, you may wish to ask for a referral to bring with you to Australia. This may allow you to join an Australian private health insurer without having to undertake waiting periods to receive some services.

Some private health insurers include: HBA www.hba.com.au, HCF www.hcf.com.au, MBF www.mbf.com.au, NIB www.nib.com.au and Medibank Private www.medibank.com.au.

Useful things to do, join and obtain

Pre-book accommodation

If you know when you are arriving in Australia or at a particular place in Australia you might wish to pre-book accommodation. For those arriving from overseas you may wish to book accommodation for at least a week, possibly two, after your arrival. I say this because by the time you have recovered from jetlag and done some sightseeing the week will be almost up. It is advisable to book if you are arriving during school holidays – especially the summer holiday, which begins mid-December and lasts until the end of January. See the Accommodation section for information on finding both short-term and long-term accommodation.

Join hostel associations

If you intend to stay in hostels during your travels around Australia it is highly suggested you join the hostel chains. The largest is YHA (Youth Hostel Association), although Australia has a number of smaller chains. See the Accommodation section for more information on hostels.

Pre-book travel

One reason for overseas travellers to pre-book your travel within Australia is that some travel passes (namely air passes) are cheaper when they are bought outside Australia.

A reason not to pre-book is that when you get to Australia, you might find your pass isn't suitable for what you want to do anymore. Perhaps you have met other travellers and want to change your plans.

Air, train and bus passes are available for purchase so I suggest you ask your travel agent about them. Also have them run through the conditions with you and find out what flexibility the passes offer – e.g. If you do change your mind in Australia can you re-route your ticket? If you don't want to use the pass, can you obtain a refund?

There are plenty of travel options available to you once you're in Australia. See the Travel options section in our Playing chapter.

To pre-book or not to pre-book? This is a question only you can answer. By booking in advance you will know how much time and money you have left to play with.

International driver's licence

It is recommended that overseas visitors obtain an International Driver's licence. Some car rental companies prefer you have one, and it is required if you buy a car.

Reciprocal roadside motor service

If overseas visitors plan to buy a car in Australia, you can apply for a CMC (Commonwealth Motoring Card) from your motoring service that will allow you to receive reciprocal motoring help from Australia's associations. Make sure you bring proof of membership from your organisation.

Collect air miles

Collecting air miles has become very popular in Australia. QANTAS has a frequent flyer club of its own which is linked with many overseas airlines. You might want to join one of these clubs because just the long flight to Australia should accumulate a few points for you. If you travel a lot by plane in Australia, you will also build up your points. Look out for other schemes offering points.

Discount cards

There are a number of discount cards available entitling you to various discounts on travel, accommodation, museum entrance fees and benefits in some 90 countries including Australia.

Full-time students can obtain the **International Student Identity Card (ISIC).** Teachers can obtain the **International Teacher Identity Card (ITIC).** Travellers 25 years old and younger, and who are not full-time students, can obtain the **International Youth Travel Card (IYTC).**

These cards are available at a number of student and youth travel agencies including STA Travel and via the **International Student Travel Confederation's (ISTC)** website www.istc.org.

Another international recognised identification and discount card is the **International Student Exchange (ISE)** card. It costs US$25 to obtain and is valid for one year. This card offers many discounts similar to cards issued by ISTC such as 10% discount on bus passes. For more details visit www.isecards.com.

Senior travellers are eleigible for a **Seniors Concession Card** allowing them discounts on travel, entrance to many places and other things.

Get fit

Get fit for your holiday – WHY? Travelling in Australia often involves outdoor activities. Do you want to climb Ayers Rock? (The Aboriginal name is Uluru.) It can take a couple of hours and is rather strenuous. If you don't climb it, you can always walk around the base, just a mere 9km. Do you want to learn to dive? You need to pass a medical for that.

Other things you might like to try include renting a push bike, exploring caves, swimming at the beach or bush walking. There is plenty to do in Australia and if you're reasonably fit, you should be able to enjoy those things you want to do.

Duty Free

It is likely you'll want to obtain duty-free items. You are permitted to bring in one litre of alcohol, 250 cigarettes, any reasonable amount of perfume as long as it's for personal use and A$400 worth of other goods. This amount is really for returning Australians who may have to pay a duty on the goods. If you bring in a very expensive item like a camera, you shouldn't have to pay duty on it as long as you intend taking it out of the country with you when you go. Do bring ownership papers or a receipt with you. More information on what you can and cannot bring into Australia can be obtained from the **Australian Quarantine and Inspection Service (AQIS)** www.aqis.gov.au.

Staying in touch

Email

Email is a cheap and efficient way to stay in touch with family and friends while travelling. You simply set up a free account with an Email service provider and then pop into an Internet café, access your account, and send and retrieve your Email. Free Email accounts can be obtained from:

Hotmail: www.hotmail.com
Yahoo: www.yahoo.com
Gmail: www.gmail.com

Mobile phone

Mobile phones are a fantastic way to keep in contact. If you are coming from overseas then contact your current provider and ask about international roaming. If you feel the fees are to high then you can always purchase a new mobile phone once you arrive in Australia or buy a new SIM. There are many places to buy mobile phones that have very competitive pricing packages. It is very easy to stay in touch by sending regular SMSs to family and friends to let them know you are safe and having a fabulous time.

Internet sites

Many travellers like to post their holiday snaps and information about the places they have seen on their own website page. This includes such sites as Facebook.

Skype is software that helps you make free PC to PC calls from your computer. It is free to other people on Skype and offers great rates to phones and mobiles around the world. For details visit www.skype.com.

Post

If you want to give people an address to contact you, then you can use Poste Restante.

Poste Restante is the term used for general delivery at any post office worldwide. An example would be:

Sharyn McCullum
Poste Restante
Sydney GPO NSW 2000

To collect the mail you will need to show some form of identification. The mail is usually kept for one month.

Mail holding services

Landbase Australia is a mail forwarding service. Jan Baetz, a yachtie, began the service for other yachties who were sailing around the world and needed a permanent address. She now provides the service to anyone.

Basically you can use Landbase Australia as your address. All your mail can be sent to them and held by them until you provide them with a forwarding address.

You will need to register with Landbase Australia to use the service.

Landbase Australia www.ozemail.com.au/~lbase/
Locked Bag 25
Gosford NSW 2250
Tel: 0408 686461 (0900 – 1700 Monday to Friday)
Fax: (02) 4323 7326
Email: lbase@ozemail.com.au

Checklist

❏ Passport and visas in order
❏ Recorded passport number
❏ Booked air ticket
❏ Signed power of attorney
❏ Made a will
❏ Taken out holiday insurance
❏ Looked into Medicare and private health insurance cover
❏ Worked out money, opened bank account
❏ Enquired about international roaming for your mobile
❏ Had vaccinations if needed
❏ Had check-up by doctor, dentist, etc.
❏ Have all doctor's referrals and required medication
❏ Pre-booked accommodation for arrival
❏ Pre-booked travel arrangements
❏ International Driver's Licence
❏ Commonwealth Motoring Card
❏ Joined hostel associations
❏ Joined air mile club/s
❏ Obtained International Youth Card/Student card
❏ Joined mail holding services
❏ Updated CV, obtained all necessary references and important documents (copied onto a USB stick)
❏ Had your qualifications recognised and registered with appropriate body
❏ Backpack/suitcase packed and labelled
❏ Bought activity to occupy yourself on plane
❏ Cancelled milk and papers
❏ Cancelled utilities: electricity, water, gas, cable TV, etc.
❏ Advised your new address to credit card company, loan manager, magazine subscriptions, friends and relatives, etc.
❏ Opened an email address

❏ Left a copy of itinerary
❏ Remember departure tax if your country has one
❏ Taken a pen to fill out landing card
❏ Arranged cash for transport from the airport

Arriving in Australia (for overseas visitors)

As a number of oceans and seas surround Australia, there are only two ways overseas visitors can arrive. That is by sea or air.

Arriving by sea vessel

For those who arrive in Australia by ocean liner or freighter, the master/captain of your vessel will radio ahead to your port of entry to advise of your arrival to begin customs and quarantine procedures.

Cruise passengers should receive a passenger declaration card to fill out prior to departing the vessel. Sometimes customs and quarantine officials will board the vessel to conduct procedures before allowing you to disembark.

If you're arriving on a small vessel, the captain must first call a Proclaimed Port of Entry (various ports along the coastline) a few hours before arrival so customs, quarantine, and immigration formalities can be put into motion.

If you are the captain or master it is compulsory for you to forward a completed Quarantine Pre-arrival report for vessels (Pratique) form (QPAR) to AQIS (Australian Quarantine and Inspection Service) prior to arriving at your first Australian port. Also, an AQIS Ballast Water Uptake/Discharge Log and Ballast Water Treatment/Exchange Log will be required to be completed and presented upon request. Once on shore, welcome to Australia.

Arriving by plane

All travellers entering Australia, including Australians returning home, must fill in a Travellers' Statement and an Incoming Passenger Card. The Travellers' Statement asks questions relating to customs and quarantine, like: are you bringing any plants, animals, illegal substances, etc. into the country? Have you exceeded duty-free allowances? You should be honest in case you are searched. The Incoming Passenger Card asks for your vital details such as name, passport number, date of birth, etc. Airline staff hand out these forms on the plane a few hours prior to your arrival. Sometimes your travel agent will give them to you.

When the plane has completely stopped you are required to remain on the plane to be sprayed. Officials from the Australian Quarantine and Inspection Service board the plane, line you up along the aisles and with your arms in the air and your legs apart, spray your every nook and cranny to kill any germs you might have brought with you. No, no, I'm just kidding about this! But officials from Australian Quarantine do board the plane. While you are still seated, they or the airline staff walk down the aisle releasing a spray from aerosol cans which eliminates any nasties on the plane. This is done because large numbers of insects become hitch-hikers on aircraft each year. Eggs, larvae and mature bugs can be found not only in passenger cabins, flight decks and galleys but also in the luggage and freight compartments and even on the exterior of the fuselage. Therefore, to stop them colonising in Australia it is necessary to spray them.

So if the person next to you shrivels up and disappears with a squeal and a pop don't worry about it. No, no, just kidding again. It is harmless to humans, although for a couple of seconds it can be a little unpleasant. You might want to look down and/or maybe cover your nose and mouth. It's not that we don't trust you but we are very strict about what is brought into the country and this ultimately benefits us all.

Once you're off the plane, follow the signs or everybody else to the Entry Control Point where you will hand over your travellers' statement, incoming passenger card and passport to a customs official.

If you are a working holiday maker you may like to have at hand any proof the official might require, like a bank statement (to prove you can support yourself during your initial stay) or a return ticket. They don't usually check these items but be prepared in case they do.

If asked about your visit, and you are here on a working holiday remember that you are on a holiday first and only hope to find casual work to further your travels around the country. Don't say 'I've come to find work' because that is not what the Working Holiday Visa is about. If you are arriving on a visitor/tourist visa never say 'I am hoping to find work' because this visa does not allow you to work while in Australia. It only allows you to holiday.

Along with your passport you will be given back your travellers' statement form which you should keep handy.

Next, collect your luggage from the carousels – hopefully you won't have too long to wait.

After picking up your luggage, head to the exit points. The green channel if you have no goods to declare, or the red channel if you do have goods to declare. At the beginning of the channels you will hand over your travellers' statement to a customs official, who will instruct you to proceed through or send you to an area for your goods to be checked. Once through, welcome to Australia.

Arriving at Sydney Airport (SYD)

Sydney is the most popular arrival destination. Sydney's Kingsford-Smith International Airport www.sydneyairport.com.au is named after Sir Charles Kingsford-Smith, who forged his way into Australian history books by pioneering long distance air travel.

The airport is situated at Mascot (locals often refer to it as Mascot airport) with the runways built into Botany Bay. There are two terminals, the international and the domestic, so make sure you go to the right one for future flights. They are linked by bus and train if you accidentally make a blunder and arrive at the wrong terminal for your flight.

Those arriving on an international flight will, of course, arrive at the international terminal. Because the airport is built in the Sydney Metropolitan Area it has a curfew and is open from 6am to 11pm. Most international flights are timed to arrive in the morning and leave in the afternoon. If several flights land at the airport in the morning (which is usually the case), and yours is one of them, be prepared for a wait to get through immigration and customs.

There are two levels to the terminal; arrivals are downstairs and departures upstairs. Before you leave the international terminal you might wish to visit the information centre and pick up all the accommodation and sightseeing brochures, free backpacker magazines and papers that you can carry. If you haven't booked any accommodation, there are accommodation boards where you can choose your accommodation, contact them and hopefully be snoozing very soon.

If you don't have anyone to greet you or a pre-arranged lift, you will want to get to your accommodation as soon as possible.

Transport from Sydney Airport

Taxi

Both terminals have their own sheltered taxi rank with on-hand supervisors during peak hours to ensure a smooth flow of taxis. Help with baby capsules, wheelchair access, maxi taxis for groups, five seaters, etc. can be organised by one of the kerbside supervisors.

A taxi fare will vary as to how far you are travelling. Throw in traffic and you are looking at paying about A$50 into the city, about A$65 to get to North Sydney and about A$90 to head south to Cronulla. A A$2.50 airport toll is also payable by all passengers taking a taxi from any of Sydney Airport's taxi ranks.

Bus

There are many bus services operating to and from Sydney Airport, most of which require pre-booking.

Public Bus services are operated by Sydney Buses: www.sydneybuses.info.

Train

Another option is to take the **Airport Rail Link** www.airportlink. com.au. The Airport Link stations are conveniently located below the airport terminals both at the International and Domestic terminals. They have been specifically located close to the baggage reclaim area for those flying into Sydney and are only a few minutes away from check-in counters for those leaving Sydney. Trains run on average every 10 minutes during the day and 15 minutes at night and only take about 15 minutes to arrive in the city. The rail link also offers connections to all Sydney Suburban and Intercity Lines.

Car

Cars can be rented at the airport. All the major car rental firms have a booth. Request a map and directions to your destination.

Arriving at Melbourne Airport (MEL)

Melbourne Airport www.melbourneairport.com.au is found in the suburb of Tullamarine and is often referred to as Tullamarine Airport. It comprises of three terminals, two domestic and one international which are all inter-linked. All terminals are well serviced by public transport.

Transport from Melbourne Airport

Bus
Skybus www.skybus.com.au offers a shuttle bus service from the airport to Melbourne CBD and city hotels. The service is available 24 hours a day, seven days a week with buses running every 10-15 minutes throughout the day and every 30-60 minutes overnight. They can be caught from outside the arrivals level of each terminal. It currently costs A$16 or A$26 return.

Taxi
Taxis are available from the ground floor level of Melbourne Airport, outside the International Terminal and both domestic Terminals. Expect a taxi fare of around A$40 for a trip into the CBD. A A$2 taxi parking fee applies per vehicle to passengers leaving Melbourne Airport from a taxi rank.

Arriving at Brisbane Airport (BNE)

Brisbane Airport www.bne.com.au is located just 20 minutes from the CBD by train. It has both an International terminal and a domestic terminal and is open 24 hours a day with no curfew.

Transport from Brisbane Airport

Taxi

Taxis are readily available outside the airport with a fare to Brisbane CBD costing around A$35 plus a A$3 fee for departing taxis only.

Train

The airport is serviced by a train that only takes 22 minutes to arrive in Brisbane City. An adult fare costs A$13 one-way. More details on the train can be obtained at www.airtrain.com.au.

Bus

Coachtrans operate services into Brisbane and to the Gold Coast. They leave at regular intervals. For bookings ring (07) 3238 4700 or book on-line at www.coachtrans.com.au.

Sun-air bus services the Sunshine Coast with daily services costing around A$45 one way. For bookings call (07) 5477 0888 or book on-line at www.sunair.com.au.

Arriving at Perth Airport (PER)

Perth Airport www.perthairport.com is Australia's fourth largest airport and is located only 12km from the heart of Perth. It has a three terminals where domestic and international flights from Europe and Africa arrive each day.

Transport from Perth Airport

Taxi

Taxis are available outside each terminal and depending on which terminal you are leaving from it costs around A$26-$35 from the airport into the heart of Perth.

Airport shuttle bus

The Perth Airport City Shuttle has several convenient drop-off and pick-up points located near hotels, motels and hostels in Perth, including Northbridge, the Central City, East Perth, West Perth, Mill Point Road and Great Eastern Highway. A fair costs A$15 one-day from the domestic terminal and A$20 one-day from the international terminal into Perth.

If you are heading to Fremantle you can catch the Fremantle Airporter. Visit their website for details www.fremantleairports-huttle.com.au.

Once you've arrived
(for working holiday makers)

There are a few formalities that are necessary for working holiday makers. It is strongly suggested that you spend a day doing these to get them out of the way so you can begin to live, work and play in Australia.

Pick up a map of the city

Pick up a map of the city you're in so you can find your way around! Your accommodation might have a free one, or go to an information centre.

If you're settling into long-term accommodation, you may wish to obtain a street directory with a more extensive listing of streets. These can be bought from newsagents, bookshops and some petrol stations.

Purchase a mobile phone

Staying in touch and being able to be reached is very important. While travelling around a mobile phone will come in very handy. It will be particularly useful so employers can contact you when they have work for you. A mobile will also be useful to help you organise your new life.

Apply for a Tax File Number (TFN)

A TFN is extremely important to your existence in Australia as all workers MUST have one. If you don't, 48% (which is the highest tax rate) of your salary will be taken in tax – instead of 29%. So it is worth your while to get this number unless you plan to work illegally! Also, banks require it to finalise your bank account.

You will need an application form to apply for this number and these are available from any tax office however, many employers can provide you with this form. Applications can be mailed but this means that original documents (i.e. your passport) must be sent with the application in order to prove your identity. The TFN can take about 28 days to come through, therefore it is suggested that you go into a tax office and apply in person so you can keep your documents. You may need them to register for work or open a bank account.

Take your passport and International Driver's Licence for proof of identification to a tax office to apply for the TFN. You can call 13 28 63 (in Australia) for the nearest office. Or have a look at the website www.ato.gov.au for more details.

When you begin a new job you'll need to advise your employer of your tax file number so they can tax you correctly. If you don't have one, they usually give you a few weeks' grace to supply them with it. If you don't, you will be taxed accordingly.

Open a bank account

The next thing on your agenda is to claim your account or open a bank account if you haven't already done so from home.

Most Australian employers will directly credit salaries into bank accounts. Therefore, if you are intending to work in Australia, you will definitely need a bank account.

To help assist with the detection of criminal activity and tax evasion the Australian Government introduced the Financial Transaction Reports Act 1988. As part of this Act, the government has imposed strict customer identification regulations on all financial institutions. This means that when you open a bank account you must show sufficient identification to the value of 100 points. Once you have achieved the 100 points, the institution will allow you to open an account.

If you are an overseas visitor, you should try to open an account within the first six weeks of your arrival. This is because your entry stamp in your passport is deemed to be equivalent to the 100 points required to open an account. If you open your account after the six-week period, you will be required to undertake the 100-point check.

Items that will give you the 100 points include passport, birth certificate, driver's licence (international/foreign), credit card, social security cards, etc. If you waited until after the six-week period, you should contact the financial institution for a description of suitable identification documents. You will also need your TFN to finalise the account otherwise the bank can deduct tax from any interest paid.

The four major banks, with many branches spread throughout Australia, are:

ANZ www.anz.com.au
Commonwealth Bank or CBA www.commbank.com.au
National Australia Bank www.national.com.au
Westpac www.westpac.com.au

Their various services are all competitive. There are other banks and building societies as well so shop around.

Most people open an interest-bearing savings or cheque account with an ATM card attached so they can operate the account at ATMs and through EFTPOS facilities.

Medicare Card

Those from the UK, New Zealand, Sweden, the Netherlands, Finland, Malta and Italy might wish to register for a Medicare card. There is a brochure available at Medicare offices if you wish to read more about the reciprocal medical arrangements. It isn't necessary to register but you never know if/when you'll get sick so it might be best to register in case it's ever needed.

Find accommodation

If you hope to find long-term accommodation (see the Accommodation section) it would be wise to begin looking before you start work as, once you're at work you might not be able to use a phone for contacting possible abodes. If you do find a place, you may also need someone at home to let in the personnel connecting gas, electricity and phone services.

Contents insurance

If you are setting up home in Australia, you should consider taking out insurance to cover your possessions. If you are buying a car, you will also need car insurance and may want to register with a motoring organisation.

Free backpacker magazines

Pick up copies of backpacker magazines. They are all free publications and are available from hostels, train and bus terminals, airports, travel clubs and agencies. They all provide information on accommodation, work opportunities and travel options throughout Australia. One magazine, British Balls, brings UK residents the latest football results. These include:

Aussie Backpacker www.aussiebackpacker.com.au
British Balls www.britishballs.com
Go West www.gowesthandbook.com
Safari Pete www.safaripete.com
TNT Magazine www.tntdownunder.com
The Word www.thewordaustralia.com.au

Useful Information

Aboriginal Australia – Aborigines have inhabited Australia for more than 40 000 years. Few other Australians or visitors know or understand much about their culture because much of their history has never been written down. What we do think about are their paintings, their dancing, their food, their didgeridoo playing and their Dreamtime.

You may see some Aborigines in the major cities but most live in the outback areas of the Northern Territory, northern Queensland and Western Australia.

Land rights are a big issue in Australia. In 1992 the High Court passed a ruling which set aside the annexation of Australia as Terra Nullius (empty land). This acknowledged that the Aborigines were the first inhabitants of this land and their rights to their traditional lands had not been extinguished. Claims for land to be handed back to the original owners are in progress.

ANZAC Day – ANZAC stands for Australian and New Zealand Army Corps and 25 April each year is a day of remembrance for the Australian and New Zealand diggers (soldiers) killed in the wars. There are dawn services and marches all over the country followed by games of two-up (the only day it is legally allowed to be played) and drinks with mates at RSL (Returned Soldiers' League) clubs.

Aussie tucker – British settlers brought their favourite fare to these shores so roast lamb, beef or chicken dinners, fish and chips, and scones with jam and cream are on the menu. Bushmen invented damper bread and billy tea.

Other tucker includes lamingtons, neenish tarts, pavlova, Vegemite, Paddle Pops, Cherry Ripes, Violet Crumbles, meat pies and sauce, witchetty grubs, kangaroo, crocodile, macadamia nuts, Iced Vovos, Chicko Rolls, and hamburgers with salad, beetroot and barbecue sauce – I'm sure you'll enjoy finding out for yourself what they taste like. As Australia is very multicultural, there are a lot of cuisines around to try.

Barbecues are a popular pastime. If you are invited to one, the norm is to BYO (bring your own) meat and grog (alcohol). The host/hostess supplies the salads, bread and some soft drink. Don't be surprised if the males hover around the barbie to advise the host on how to cook while the females offer the hostess help in the kitchen. Usually the hostess has everything under control, so the guests can socialise or laugh at the men barbecuing.

Redheads shouldn't be offended if called **blue/bluey** – it's just a nickname.

Going to the **beach** is an extremely popular pastime, yet many people (Australians and visitors) are dragged from the sea each year because they didn't adhere to beach safety. The important thing to remember is that you must swim between the flags. Surf lifesavers who have spent many years in and on the water carefully mark out and patrol these safe swimming areas.

Rips (strong currents) are a very dangerous hazard to swimmers and it's easy to be dragged out to sea if you get caught in one. If you do get caught, do not panic and do not swim against the rip as you will just tire yourself out. Swim across the rip, parallel to the beach. If you find yourself in serious trouble, raise your hand high in the air and call for help.

Beware of waves known as 'dumpers'. These waves hurtle you underneath them before dumping you on the ocean floor. They can hurt immensely.

Remember to use exorbitant amounts of sunscreen as the "lobster" look isn't that great. Wear a hat, sunglasses and T-shirt and drink plenty of water.

If learning to surf or body board, get lessons from a professional organisation. Regular classes are offered throughout the year. Surf shops in the surf areas should be able to advise where to organise your lessons.

Bushfires are a regular occurrence in hot weather and unfortunately some are deliberately lit. To help reduce their severity, controlled burns are undertaken during the winter months. If you are camping, make sure your fire is extinguished by throwing dirt on it. Don't throw cigarette butts out of car windows. If there is a fire and you are in your car, find an open area off the road (in case fire engines come blazing through), stay in the car, wind up the windows, close the air vents, get below window level, cover yourself and wait until the fire passes. Don't touch any metal as it might be hot; use a piece of material to open the door. It is preferable to evacuate early if you are travelling on foot.

Bushrangers per se do not exist but during the late 1800s they roamed Australia, leaving a legacy as folk heroes. Ned Kelly is Australia's most famous bushranger. See his death mask, armour and where he was hanged at the Melbourne Gaol, or the site of his last gun battle in Glenrowan, Victoria.

Clothes – Dressing in Australia is of a casual nature. During hot weather most people wear cool, loose fitting, shorts and T-shirts, dresses, etc. City people dress differently from country folk who favour jeans, shirts and Akubra hats.

The **currency** is simple and based on the decimal system of 100 cents to the dollar. The one and two cent coins have been phased out but things can still cost, say, 98c. When this happens the price is either rounded up or down to the nearest 5 cents.

The silver coins are the 5c, 10c, 20c and 50c pieces. Then there are the gold $1 and $2 coins. Paper notes have been phased out and replaced with polymer notes, which are the pinky-purple $5 note, the blue $10 note, the orange $20 note, the gold $50 note and the grey $100 note. All the notes honour famous Australians.

Some shopkeepers don't like receiving $50 or $100 notes if you are buying something small as it can take all their change.

Cyclones are common in the summer months in tropical North

Queensland, the Northern Territory and the northern region of Western Australia.

Dates are written with the day first, then the month, then the year. Australia has some of the **deadliest creatures** in the world.

- Bees – Those lovely little critters that make our honey can cause an allergic reaction in some. If you're stung remove the sting by scraping it out, clean the wound and apply a cold compress. Seek medical help if an allergic reaction occurs.
- Wasps – Unlike bees, wasps often sting several times. They are attracted to sweet drinks and meat being cooked so watch out for them at those barbies. Apply a cold compress and seek medical help if an allergic reaction occurs.
- Blue-ringed octopus – You'll find this octopus living in rock pools on the beach. They are harmless when left alone but if they're disturbed vivid blue rings appear on their skin. A bite from one of these can be fatal so seek medical help urgently. It is advisable to leave them alone.
- Cone shells – Those shells you often pick up while walking on reefs may be cone shells. They have deadly stingers which come out the bottom of the shell. If you're stung, pour vinegar over the sting and seek medical help.
- Crocodiles – There are two types of crocodile, the saltwater and freshwater. Both are found in Far North Queensland and the Northern Territory. Salties (saltwater) are very dangerous. Freshies (freshwater) are usually harmless if left alone, so they say, although I wouldn't trust them. I've heard that if one comes at you, you should run away in a zig-zag pattern because they can't run that way – I haven't tested this theory out and I don't plan to.
- Sharks – There are sharks all around the coastline of Australia. They like to feed during sunrise and sunset.

  Most patrolled beaches have shark nets to keep them out and an alarm will go off to get everyone out of the water if one is spotted. Helicopters will often come in to herd it/them back out to sea. If a shark comes at you, hit it on the nose as apparently that's its vulnerable spot. I haven't tested this theory out either. If you're bitten, stem the flow of blood by applying pressure to the wound and seek medical help.

- Snakes are more scared of us than we are of them, so if you encounter one, stand still or back away slowly.

  It is against the law to run over them on purpose if you see one slithering on the road. If you are bitten, take note of what it looks like so the correct anti-venom can be given. Don't suck out or wash off the venom as if you don't recognise what type of snake bit you, the venom will help in identifying it. Immobilise the entire limb with a pressure bandage and splint, and seek medical advice.

- Spiders are found all around Australia.

  Funnel Webs can be found around Sydney, on the NSW coast and in south-east Queensland. I strongly advise you not to go looking for them as their bite is very painful and deadly. They are big spiders about 2 or 3 cm in length – well, I call that big – and are black or reddish brown. If bitten, seek urgent medical attention.

  Redback spiders are identifiable by the red markings on their back. They are small black spiders with a big bite and live in most parts of Australia. Give boots and gloves a shake before you put them on. When camping, check your sleeping bag before you get in.

- Stingers/jellyfish/blue bottles All these creatures are predominantly found in coastal waters during the warmer months. Their stings can cause great pain and leave welts on the skin. If possible, flood the sting with vinegar as that neutralises the tentacles enough for you to gently pick them off. Applying ice can relieve the pain. Seek medical help.

- Stonefish – Watch out for these while walking in shallow tropical waters. As the name suggests they look like stones but are actually fish with very painful, poison-bearing spikes on their back. Wear shoes or thongs when wading in water. If you step on a stonefish, remove the spikes and seek medical help.

• Ticks live all around Australia. They are either oval or round and flat but when engorged with blood they increase in size. They hide in body crevices or in your hair and can cause paralysis. Pull them out with tweezers and seek medical advice if you find any on your body.

A **departure tax** is required to leave Australia but as of 1 July 1995 it has been included in the price of your ticket.

Disability awareness is increasing in Australia, but there is still a long way to go. Legislation requires new accommodation to meet accessibility standards however, there are many old establishments where modifications have not been made. Many key tourist attractions are now providing access for those with limited mobility and some are addressing the needs of visitors with other impairments. Tour operators are offering accessible vehicles as they aren't allowed to discriminate against potential customers with disabilities.

A very useful website for planning your holiday if you have a disability is www.e-bility.com/travel/. This website provides lots of information on tour operators and accommodation for disabled travellers.

The Tourism Australia website www.australia.com also has useful information which you can access if you look under 'Plan Your Trip', then 'Special Interest Travel', then 'Disabled Travellers'.

Drinking – To drink alcohol in licensed premises you must be over 18.

Beers on tap are served in a glass. Glasses vary in size and can be called different names in different areas. For example, a 'schooner' in NSW is known as a 'pot' in Queensland. You can also buy 'middies'. If you're unsure of the size just ask for a beer and the bar person will usually pick up a glass and say 'This size?' You don't have to return a glass to be refilled as you are given a new glass for each drink.

Beer can also be bought as a 'tinnie' or 'tube' which means in a can. It's a little uncouth for girls to drink from a can – besides, I think it tastes different.

You can also buy beer in bottles of varying sizes. Most are 'twisties', meaning capped with a twist top. Don't use your teeth to open them. If you are having a party you can buy a keg.

Beers are served ice-cold. After a long hot day you'll know why. Be careful not to leave your finger tips or lips behind on the glass.

Each state produces its own beer, such as Swan Lager in WA, Tooheys in NSW, VB (Victorian Bitter) in Victoria, and XXXX in Queensland, but there are new beers hitting the market all the time.

You can find a drink in pubs, RSL clubs, Leagues clubs, trade union clubs (you may have to join the clubs and dress nicely, including shoes), nightclubs and restaurants.

Pubs also serve counter meals which are good value. On Friday nights they often have raffles with meat trays, vegetables and chooks (chickens) on offer for prizes.

Many pubs have beer gardens, which are nice to sit in with a cold drink or a meal on a warm day.

Drivers follow the left-hand side of the road. All major roads are sealed while minor roads can have a dirt surface. Some roads have a single lane of tar seal, and when a car approaches from the other direction you will need to move off the seal to pass each other. Many roads are named after explorers.

Speed limits are in kilometres. In built-up areas you can usually travel at 60km per hour. Near schools you can do 40km, while on the open road it's 100km per hour. There are road signs to tell you the speed, but speeds can vary from state to state. For example, in the Northern Territory you can only do 25km an hour in public places or off-street car parks.

For those who might have bought an old car which only shows miles on the speedometer, convert your speed to kilometres by using this rough formula: divide miles by five, then multiply by eight to get kilometres. Here's an example: you're driving 50 miles an hour, divide by five = 10, then multiply by eight = 80km per hour. To save your brain, 60km = 37.5 miles; 40km = 25 miles; and 100km = 62.5 miles.

It is compulsory to wear a seatbelt in both the front and back seats. If you drive with one arm leaning out the window put suntan lotion on it, or wear a long-sleeved shirt.

If someone flashes their lights at you it usually means something is wrong with your own lights, or that there are police ahead. It is illegal to advise others that police are ahead but people still do it.

Watch out for roundabouts. The main rule is to give way to the right and only enter when it is clear. If you are turning left or going straight through stay in the left lane. If you're turning right, stay in the right lane.

When driving long distances, make sure you have adequate rest breaks and if possible share the driving.

Don't drink and drive as there are stiff penalties. Random breath testing units, known as booze buses, can appear anywhere.

Road rules can vary from state to state, including the speed limit so pick up a set of Interstate Road Rules from a motor authority.

Driving in the outback – Make sure your vehicle is prepared for the outback. Have it fully checked over before setting out. Take spare tyres, food, plenty of water and fuel and if you break down stay with the vehicle. Off the main road, property owners never ignore smoke – burn a tyre maybe. If you are going really off-road, advise someone, such as the police or the hostel, where you are going and when you expect to arrive.

Motoring organisations have information available to their members about driving in the outback and equipping the car for such trips. Ask for information when you visit to obtain maps, etc.

If you are planning to go off-road, find out if you will be travelling through Aboriginal land, because you will need a special permit to enter the area. Tours have this special permission.

Outback tracks

There are a number of outback routes you may wish to venture on, but ensure you have a fully equipped 4WD to do so.

Birdsville Track runs from Marree in South Australia to Birdsville in Queensland. It is 517km long and is an old droving trail.

Canning Stock Route This route is an old cattle-droving trail that is some 1700km-long and runs southwest from Halls Creek to Wiluna in WA. The trail crosses the Great Sandy Desert and Gibson Desert and is unmaintained. You will need a well-equipped 4WD to undertake this route.

Oodnadatta Track This track virtually runs parallel to the old Ghan railway line. It is around 429km long and runs from Marree to Oodnadatta.

Strzelecki Track This track covers much the same area as the Birdsville Track. It starts at Marree and goes to Innamincka, where Burke and Wills, two of Australia's explorers died.

Eating out – Backpackers/budget travellers rarely dine out; it's a good cheap feed you're after to sustain your travelling.

Look out for cafés and BYO restaurants. Food halls in shopping centres have a variety of cheap eateries. The corner milk bar makes hamburgers, fish and chips, etc. RSL clubs, trade union clubs and football clubs all have restaurants/bistros which serve good meals. You may have to join one of them, but it might be worth it to get a decent feed.

Australia is a very multicultural country so there are a lot of cuisines to try including Chinese, Thai, Japanese, Mexican, Indian, Italian, etc. There are 'cheap eat' books available if you are serious about eating lots at little cost.

Eucalyptus oil is highly flammable which is why the Australian bush, having so many eucalyptus trees, is highly combustible.

In an **emergency** dial **000** for the Police, Ambulance or Fire Brigade.

Native **fauna** includes koalas, kangaroos, wallabies, wombats, platypuses, bilbies, possums, quokkas, echidnas and dingoes. There are many birds including the kookaburra, emu and a range of parrots and cockatoos. They can be seen in zoos, wildlife parks or better still, in their native environment.

Australia is an extremely popular destination for **gay** and **lesbian** travellers. This is largely due to events such as the Sydney Gay & Lesbian Mardi Gras www.mardigras.org.au held annually in February and March. Melbourne's Midsumma Festival www.midsumma.org.au held mid-January to mid-February and Adelaide's Feast www.feast.org.au held in November.

All the major Australian cities have gay newspapers with relevant advertisements and information. There are also a number of lifestyle magazines including *Lesbians on the Loose*, *DNA*, *Women out West* and city-based magazines like *Adelaide's Blaze*.

There are a number of useful websites to help you organise your travel, they include:

Gay and Lesbian Tourism Australia www.galta.com.au which offers general information and **Queer Australia** www.queeraustralia.com.au.

The **GST (Goods and Services Tax)** was introduced to Australia in 2000. At going to press the rate is 10 per cent.

The **heat and humidity** can affect people in different ways with symptoms of dizziness, nausea, vomiting, difficulty breathing, rapid pulse, etc. Drink plenty of water or energy drinks if you feel washed out. Try to stay cool. Sunstroke can occur when your body's heat regulating system breaks down and you fail to sweat.

Lingo (language) is quite unique. Many words have letters not pronounced, or words have been shortened, e.g.:

'ang on	wait a minute
arvo	afternoon
'avago	have a go
banana bender	a person from Queensland
barra	barramundi (a type of fish)
barrack	supporting your team (don't say 'root' in Oz, this is an expression for sex)
beyond the black stump / back of Bourke	a remote area
blowie	blow fly
bludger	lazy person
blue heeler	cattle dog
bonza	good, great
booze bus	police breath testing unit
(you've got) Buckley's	you've got no chance
give it a burl	give it a go
BYO/G	bring your own/grog
capsicum	pepper
chook	chicken
chuck a U-ee	do a U-turn
chunder / chuck / spew	vomit
clobber	clothes
cobber	friend (rarely used nowadays)
cocky	farmer, or cockatoo (bird)
cooee	a bush call
cossies	bathing costume
crow eater	a South Australian
dag	untidy or unfashionable person
dead set	really, truly, genuine
derro	tramp/homeless person
dinky-di	genuine
drongo	idiot
dunny	outside toilet

durex	in England it's sticky-tape, in Oz, it's a condom
eggplant	aubergine
Esky	a portable cooling box
fair crack of the whip	fair go
fair dinkum	really, truly, genuinely
fair go	a reasonable chance
ferals	people living 'at one' with nature
football	Rugby League, Rugby Union, AFL, soccer
Fremantle Doctor	the sea breeze in Perth
galah	a bird, or a loud, noisy person
garbo	garbage collector
full as a goog	drunk
get the guernsey	be the winner
gladwrap	cling film
grog / plonk / booze /piss	alcohol
G'day	hello
had a gutful	had enough
jig	play truant
Kiwi	person from New Zealand
loaded	wealthy or drunk
lollies	sweets
main street/main drag	high street
Mexican	someone south of the border (Queenslanders call NSW people Mexicans and NSW people call Victorians Mexicans)
mollydooker	left-handed person
no worries	no problem
in the nuddy / starkers	in the nude or naked
pokies	poker machines
postcode	zip code
prang	minor car accident

rego	car registration, MOT, road tax
sandgroper	someone from Western Australia
sangers	sandwiches
scorcher	hot day
scungies /dick-stickers / Speedos	men's swimwear
sickie (take a)	a day off from work when not sick
snags	sausages
southpaw	left-handed person
strewth	gee whiz
Strine	short for Australian (language)
Surf and turf	a meal of seafood and meat
tinnie / tube	can of beer
top drop	a good beer or wine
trots	races (usually harness/horse races), or it can mean diarrhoea
true-blue	genuine
tucker	food
two-up	illegal gambling game where two coins are tossed in the air and bets taken on whether they land heads or tails
wag	play truant, wives and girlfriends of footballers
walkabout	disappear for a while
whopper	a lie, or something larger than usual such as a wave
wobbly (chuck a)	have a temper tantrum
yakka	hard work
yobbo	uncultured person
yonks	ages ago/a long time
Yowie	fictional abominable snowman or big foot
zucchini	courgette

Australia uses the **metric system**. Speed and distance are measured in kilometres (km); temperature is in degrees Celsius (°C); weight is in kilograms (kg).

Ozzie stereotypes

- Bushie: is a person born and bred in the bush. They rarely come to the large cities. They are usually wearing Blundstone boots, Driza-Bone coats, checked shirts with jeans and an Akubra hat.
- Feral: is a person with dreadlocks, beads and wears cotton outfits. You will find them in inner-city areas and in Byron Bay, Bellingen and Nimbin.
- Ocker is a working-class Australian who usually drive utes and do blue-collar (manual) jobs. They also like to watch footie and bet at the TAB. They also like their backyard barbies.
- Surfie: is a person who loves to surf. They are tanned with sun-bleached hair.
- Westie: is someone from the western suburbs. They have gone west because it is usually cheaper to live in these suburbs.

Politics/Government is based on the British system. Queen Elizabeth II is the official head of state with her representative in Australia being the Governor-General. The Prime Minister is the leader of the government. There are three levels of government, Federal, State and Local.

Federal: The Federal Government is based in Canberra which is the administrative centre. The parliament has the House of Representatives and the Senate. Here, decisions are made on matters which affect the whole country such as tax, defence, social services, trade, etc.

State: Each Australian state and territory has its own government which is responsible for matters such as health and education, etc.

Local: Local Government is the third tier to Australia's

government. Shires, municipal or city councils are responsible for matters relating to urban and rural regions. They are responsible for such matters as town planning, garbage collection, maintaining roads, and local facilities such as libraries, etc.

Post is delivered Monday to Friday in populated areas by trusty posties on foot, on pushbikes, or motorbikes or in vans. In some remote areas deliveries might be made just once a week and could be by plane.

Post offices are open from 9am to 5pm Monday to Friday with some opening on Saturday morning.

Local mail is usually delivered the next day. Interstate mail will take 1-2 days. It currently costs 55c to send a letter within Australia.

To address a letter within Australia:

Name
Street No. then Street Name
Suburb State Postcode

The correct postcode is vital because if you get the suburb name wrong it will still get to the right place with a correct postcode.

State names are abbreviated, and each state's four-digit postcode begins with a different number:

Australian Capital Territory and	ACT	2
New South Wales	NSW	2
Northern Territory and	NT	5
South Australia	SA	5
Queensland	Qld	4
Tasmania	Tas	7
Victoria	Vic	3
Western Australia	WA	6

Public holidays

1st January	New Year's Day
26th January	Australia Day
Easter	March/April
25th April	ANZAC Day
June	Queen's Birthday (except WA)
25th December	Christmas Day
26th December	Boxing Day

Each state has various holidays.

Most **religions** are catered for, although Australia is predominantly Catholic or Church of England (Anglican). Most townships have a church or two.

Shopping hours are mostly 9am to 5.30pm Monday to Friday with late night shopping on Thursdays and Fridays in some areas. In areas that specifically cater to tourists, like the Gold Coast, shops will stay open most week nights until 9pm. They also open on a Saturday, usually until 4pm although some small places close around noon. There is also Sunday trading in some areas.

There is no sales tax added onto the things you purchase as everything has tax already incorporated into the price.

Australia has the highest incidence of **skin cancer** in the world and even though you might have a desire to lie on every beach along Australia's coastline, be sensible about it.

Make sure you rub in sunscreen with a sun protection factor (SPF) of 15+ or SPF30+. Put it on at least half an hour before you go to the beach so it absorbs into your skin. Even if it is water-resistant, you should reapply it after swimming as it can wash off.

Also wear a wide-brimmed hat and sunglasses to protect your eyes. It is preferable to cover up completely.

Stay out of the sun during the hottest hours of the day, from 10am to 2pm (during daylight saving 11am to 3pm), as those nasty burning rays are at their strongest during these times.

Even though it looks healthy to have a tan you don't have to be the brownest berry around or you may end up a wrinkly old berry. Maybe a fake tan is what you need.

Social events for the calendar – There are too many events happening throughout the country at any one time to list them all but some of the major ones are:

January: Festival of Sydney; Australia Day (26th); Australian Tennis Open in Melbourne; Tamworth Country Music Festival – a time for some real good ol' toe tapping, lasts for 10 days and culminates in the Country Music Awards; Big Day Out – loads of local and international bands playing their way around the country.

February: Gay and Lesbian Mardi Gras – not to be missed; Chinese New Year.

March: Melbourne's Moomba Festival; Adelaide Cup; Adelaide Arts Festival; Royal Easter Show in Sydney; Formula I Grand Prix in Melbourne; Coral spawning Ningaloo Reef, WA.

April: Comedy festival in Melbourne, ANZAC Day (25th); Surfing competition at Bell's Beach, Victoria.

May:

June: Sydney Film Festival – two weeks of movies at various venues; Ski season begins.

July: Darwin Beer Can Regatta; Camel Cup in Alice Springs

August: New Year's Eve ski season; City-to-Surf foot race, Sydney; Henley-on-Todd Regatta, Alice Springs.

September: Birdsville Races; winter sport finals.

October: Bathurst 1000 – car race on the Mount Panorama Circuit; Cricket season begins; Sleaze Ball; Indy Grand Prix on the Gold Coast; Iron man series, running throughout the summer, begins.

November: Melbourne Cup (first Tuesday).

December: Carols by Candlelight; Boxing Day, the beginning of the Sydney-to-Hobart Yacht – stand on the headlands or on the beaches along the coast and watch the yachts make their way to Tasmania.

Sporting mad – Australia has many sporting codes. The major spectator sports are cricket and soccer in summer and Rugby League, Rugby Union and AFL (known as 'Aussie Rules') in winter.

There is plenty of sport on TV if you can't make it to the actual ground. Many pub TVs have a sports program on, so a possible conversation starter could be: 'What's the score?'

Australia has three **time zones**, Eastern Standard Time, Central Standard Time and Western Standard Time.

Eastern Standard Time covers the eastern states of Queensland, New South Wales, Australian Capital Territory, Victoria and Tasmania and is 10 hours ahead of Greenwich Mean Time (GMT).

Central Standard Time covers South Australia and the Northern Territory and is 30 minutes behind Eastern Standard Time. So it is 9.5 hours ahead of GMT.

Western Standard Time covers all of Western Australia and is two hours behind Eastern Standard Time, 1.5 hours behind Central Standard Time and 8 hours ahead of GMT. Confused? Well, during summertime, some states have daylight saving just to confuse you even more.

New South Wales, the ACT, Victoria, Tasmania and South Australia have synchronised daylight saving, which begins on the first Sunday in October and ends the first Sunday in April. Western Australia is conducting a three-year trial of daylight saving. In 2008 it began early in October and will end on the last Sunday in March 2009. Queensland and the Northern Territory do not observe daylight saving.

Where daylight saving is being observed, clocks are turned forward one hour. EST becomes 11 hours ahead of Greenwich Mean Time. CST becomes 10.5 hours ahead of GMT and WST becomes nine hours ahead of GMT.

If you ever wanted to celebrate two New Years' Eves, now's your chance. Have one in New South Wales, then cross the border and celebrate again an hour later in Queensland.

Tipping is discretionary. If you thought the service was really good, you might want to tip about 10% of the bill, or leave the change behind. Taxi drivers are appreciative when you round up the fare.

If you are a visitor to Australia and have purchased goods worth A$300 or more within 30 days prior to your departure, you may apply to the **Tourist Refund Scheme (TRS)** for a refund of the GST paid on the goods. You can collect your cash refund from TRS booths at any international airport. For more details, visit www.customs.gov.au.

There are five main **TV** channels. The ABC (Australian Broadcasting Corporation) and SBS (which shows many foreign language films and news bulletins) are government funded, while there are three commercial networks including Channel 7, 9 and 10. Not all areas receive the channels. Pay television is also very popular in Australia.

Australia has a number of **World Heritage-listed areas**. They include Kakadu and Uluru-Kata Tjuta National Parks in the Northern Territory, the Great Barrier Reef, the Wet Tropics and Fraser Island in Queensland, Rain Forests and the Willandra Lakes Region in New South Wales, the Australian Mammal Fossil Sites in South Australia, Shark Bay in Western Australia and the Tasmanian Wilderness in Tasmania.

Moving on –
(for overseas working holiday makers)

There comes a time when your travels near an end. This can be because you are either heading home or moving on to another country. Before you do there are a few things to sort out.

Give notice

Give advance notice of your departure to a number of organisations so they can calculate final payments. Give notice to your landlord, electricity, gas, water and telephone companies (if these bills are in your name) and your employer to name a few. Notify your bank that you are leaving the country and transfer the money out of your account to one in your home country.

Income tax and superannuation refunds

When moving on you will need every cent you can get your hands on. If you have worked in Australia you should see if you are eligible for a tax and/or superannuation refund as a fat cheque will definitely come in handy for your onward journey. Contact the Australian Tax Office www.ato.gov.au or a specialist traveller tax service such as www.taxback.com or www.expresstaxback.com.au.

Forwarding things on

You may have accumulated a lot of things during your travels. Instead of purchasing extra bags that could lead to airport fees for excess baggage, you could send your things by mail or a shipping company.

Via mail

If you only have small and light parcels visit a post office to find out rates for sending parcels by air and surface mail.

Via shipping companies

Many people ship their excess baggage home. This can take anywhere from 10 to 15 weeks on a cargo ship.

Shipping companies offer two types of service: door-to-port and door-to-door.

If you opt for the door-to-port service you will be required to resolve any customs issues and visit the port to collect your luggage. Door-to-door is more expensive because included in the fee from the outset are handling charges, unloading charges, custom fees and delivery to your door.

Shop around for the best deal. Compare prices and expected delivery date. Read about insurance before taking any out to cover your luggage on its journey home.

PART II – Living in Australia

Accommodation is diverse in Australia and ranges from sleeping in a tent to staying in campervans, hostels, farm stays, B&Bs, homesteads, units, town houses, terraces, three-bedroom homes, budget hotel chains and five-star hotels. Quite a wide choice really!

Depending on your travelling situation, you will require short-term accommodation some time during your travels in Australia. As you will discover, there is plenty of short-term accommodation available to appeal to a wide variety of tastes and budgets.

Short-term accommodation

Hotels

Glossy accommodation brochures only scratch the surface of the lodgings available to you and mostly cater to those prepared to pay a day's salary for the privilege. There are a number of hotel chains in Australia that offer varying levels of accommodation in most areas including:

Best Western www.bestwestern.com.au
The Budget Motel Chain www.budgetmotelchain.com.au
Golden Chain www.goldenchain.com.au

Then, of course, you have accommodation in **Hilton Hotels** www.hilton.com.au and **Sheraton Hotels** www.sheraton.com.au.

A couple of useful websites for finding accommodation, particularly holiday accommodation, are www.lastminute.com.au and www.wotif.com.au where you can find some great deals.

Most travellers of any age, but particularly working holiday makers, will only stay in up-market places like the Hilton and the Sheraton for a little luxury, particularly if travelling on their own. Many travellers stay in hostels. In Australia there are YHA hostels and independently owned hostels.

Hostels

There are a number of hostel chains in Australia that as well as offering budget accommodation have employment links and a travel agency. The hostels also offer welcome packs usually including your accommodation for a few nights as well as 'meet and greet' at the airport, bus or train terminal, phone cards and sightseeing trips. However, you should have a look at their individual websites to see what these welcome packs include. Most of them also allow you to book online. The contact details of the hostel chains are listed further on.

What hostels offer

Most hostels have a minibus offering a courtesy lift from the bus/train/airport. When they know you are arriving they will be there to meet you. Some allow you to call at any time for a lift to the hostel as many of them advertise at the airport, bus and train information centres.

Almost all hostels include free sheets, pillow cases and blankets in the nightly price or they can be rented at minimal cost. This will save you having to carry around your own sleeping bag and sheet which hostel chains such as YHA don't let you use anyway because of strict Australian hygene standards.

Air-conditioning is something to consider, particularly when travelling in the hot summer months, especially in the Northern Territory and Far North Queensland, while central heating is appreciated in the southern states during the winter months.

Twenty-four-hour access is also important as you don't want or need curfews. Most hostels have a security system, which you will be given access to so you can enter the hostel after hours.

Other things to look out for include: help finding work; personal lockers in rooms; fully equipped clean kitchen with enough room in fridge/s to leave food; TV/common room; laundry with a soap machine, iron and ironing board; telephones; travel booking service; luggage storage facilities; safety deposit boxes; fans (if air-conditioning isn't available in hot weather) and heating in cold weather; free tea and coffee making facilities; breakfast; party nights; free once-a-week barbecue; swimming pool; bathrooms that are cleaned daily; en-suite toilets and showers; an information lounge; discounts for seven-day or longer stays; elevator to all floors; prime site e.g. near the beach; fire safe (more information further on).

So, with all that is on offer, how do you choose a hostel to stay in? Fellow travellers are a great source of advice on hostels; they can either recommend or pan one. After all, isn't that what a fellow traveller is for? To pass on useful information!

You really need to have an idea of what you want from a hostel; do you want a party hostel or a quiet one? If you read their advertisements, you can usually tell what kind of hostel they are. For instance, a small, quiet, family-run hostel should give you a good night's slept and have a communal area if you want to socialise. Other hostels advertise backpacker 'party nights' every night, so will probably be pretty noisy. Choose what suits you.

Accommodation in hostels is dormitory-style, with varying numbers of beds (bunks) in a room. The number of occupants per room can vary from four up to 12 or more. Some dorms are single sex while others can be mixed dorms. You should know what you prefer when booking or checking in. Some hostel owners (not many but there are some) have only $$$ signs in their eyes and if you don't request a bed in say, an all male four-bed dorm (if you are male or if female a four-bed female dorm), they could put you in an eight-bed mixed dorm. Generally the cheaper the room, the more people in it.

Some hostels offer single, family, double and twin rooms (which is good news if you are travelling with a special friend and only want to 'sleep' with them). Be prepared to pay extra to stay in them and note: they are limited so booking in advance, particularly in peak times, is a good idea.

Fire safety

As you travel around Australia you will discover there is a lot of hostel and backpacker/budget accommodation available. As described, they vary in quality and services. One thing that should be high on your list of priorities when choosing a hostel is whether the accommodation is fire safe.

There have been two tragic fires in Australia that have destroyed backpacker accommodation and killed a number of travellers staying in them. One was in Kings Cross, Sydney, and the other in Childers, Queensland.

It is imperative that you consider a fire-safety check before you agree to stay at a hostel. If you feel the hostel doesn't meet the following criteria, do not be afraid to leave. After all, your life is worth far more than A$20 for a dorm room! These are the main things to consider:

- Are there fire stairs and exists and are these free of obstructions?
- Are there maps in your room and others clearly showing

where the fire stairs and exists are?
- Is there a working smoke alarm fitted in your room and other areas?
- Can the fire exit doors be opened at all times during the day and night?
- Are the exit signs clearly marked?
- Is there an evacuation area if an alarm goes off?
- Are there fire hoses and extinguishers? Are these unobstructed and in working order?
- Is there an excessive amount of rubbish at the hostel, which may fan a fire?

Dorm living

Dorm living is an experience if you aren't used to it. You will be sharing with people you have never met before, but you should have a common goal – to live, work and play in Australia.

Be prepared for people changing in front of you, having little or no privacy, people coming in late and getting up early, zippers zipping, bags rustling, alarms going off, snorers, talkers and even bonkers, who are usually embarrassed in the morning.

Even though you want to travel as cheaply as possible, I have met people whose health has been affected. A male friend always seemed to have snorers in his dorm and he was becoming crankier and crankier as the days passed from lack of sleep. If this happens to you, then paying a few dollars more for your own room in a cheap hotel may be worth it for a good night's sleep.

Security in hostels

Sometimes it's not professional thieves you have to worry about, but your fellow travellers. Be careful in hostels with your personal belongings, especially your valuables. There are transients who steal things like jewellery or cameras and sell them quickly. If possible, don't keep all your valuables together or, if you do, keep them with you at all times. You should even take them to the shower with you in a water-proof bag.

When unpacking or packing your bag, try to do it when no one else is around.

Be careful with all your belongings because popular items to go missing include that expensive shampoo and conditioner you've just bought to bring life back to your hair, or that new deodorant, or that carton of milk, or that new T-shirt. Unfortunately some cheap travellers don't have any regard for other travellers' belongings and it's sad to say, but that's how they survive.

Staying healthy in hostels

As mentioned, sleep deprivation is a health hazard. So are bad eating habits.

Hostels usually have a communal kitchen for you to use. Many single travellers feel self-conscious about cooking and eating in front of others who aren't. If this is you, maybe your room mate/s might want to share a cooked meal with you. Easy things to cook include pasta dishes – a bag of pasta and a bottle of sauce can be easily bought at supermarkets and are relatively cheap. So is soup and a bread roll.

It can be very easy when you are on your own to pop into fast food establishments for a bite to eat, but try to eat healthily.

Hostel chains

There are a number of hostel chains in Australia. They are listed in alphabetical order and not in any order of preference. They include:

www.hostelaustralia.com is part of www.hostelworld.com. This site has an extensive listing of Australian hostels, which may be booked online.

HostelBookers www.hostelbookers.com is a website that allows you to book a hostel in more than 2500 destinations worldwide including Australia.

Nomads World www.nomadsworld.com is a network of high-quality hostels in Australia and other countries. You can book your stay online.

VIP Backpackers www.vipbackpackers.com provide access to hundreds of hostels around the world including Australia. VIP membership also provides discounts on travel and tours.

YHA (Youth Hostels Association) www.yha.com.au are renowned around the world for offering affordable accommodation and Australian YHA hostels are no different. They are situated in all the major cities and towns you are likely to visit on your travels around Australia and include many services.

The YHA offers clean, budget accommodation, with 24-hour access, laundry facilities, TV rooms, communal lounges and communal kitchens or bistros. One thing I liked about some of the hostels was the light above my bed. By using this light, early risers and late-night revellers do not need to disturb everyone else.

When you join the YHA, obtain its accommodation guide so you can plan your travels.

How to find hostels

Carry a copy of the hostel accommodation guides for easy reference. Aussie Backpacker magazine also has a free accommodation booklet. Also look at hostel advertisements in the backpacker magazines.

The major airports have accommodation boards where you can choose a place to stay. There is usually a free-phone service available connecting you directly to the accommodation advertised, or the people behind the information counters can advise you.

Camping/caravan/tourist parks

There are many places to camp around Australia, with many camp sites ideally located near beaches or in bush surroundings.

Facilities vary from caravan park to caravan park with many now being called a tourist park due to the fabulous facilities they offer. These can include a swimming pool, tennis court, laundry, shop or mini-mart, games room, children's playground and clean amenities blocks.

If you don't have your own tent or campervan you can still stay at camping grounds and caravan parks, as they have permanent tents, on-site vans, cabins and villas, which can sleep six to eight people. Permanent tents are on powered sites so you will be able to cook and possibly watch TV – what a luxury if you have been roughing it.

Most people who stay in camp grounds/tourist parks stay short-term (usually overnight or a week or two). However, depending on the season, many allow you to stay on a long-term basis.

It is very easy to find camping grounds/tourist parks as they are well sign posted. There are a number of chains including:

Big 4 Holiday Parks www.big4.com.au. There are about 170 holiday parks around Australia providing a range of accommodation from caravan and camping sites to first-class cabins and villas. They are all conveniently located across the country, at or near many of Australia's premier holiday destinations. They are also in selected capital city locations to provide access to all major sights, attractions and entertainment. You could join the Big 4 Club to get discounts at Big 4 holiday parks and other services.

Family Parks www.familyparks.com.au is an independent group of caravan parks and camping grounds located throughout all states and territories of Australia.

B&B (Bed and Breakfast)

The B&B concept has become popular in Australia. Types of B&B vary but all have one thing in common – they provide a warm welcome, somewhere to stay and breakfast in the morning.

Breakfast is an integral part of the tariff and is either prepared by your hosts or by way of breakfast provisions that you can prepare at your leisure.

Locations of B&Bs are as diverse as the style of B&Bs available. You will find B&Bs located by the beach, in the bush, mountains, city or rural and outback areas all around Australia. The types available include home stay, farm stay, country home, guesthouse, inn, cottage, cabin and apartments.

Some useful websites to visit include:

Bed & Breakfast Australia www.bedandbreakfast.com.au, which has a listing of bed and breakfast establishments around Australia.

www.bbbook.com.au is a great website listing literally hundreds of B&Bs around Australia. It is backed up with a printed book.

Farm stays

For a truly memorable Aussie experience you may be interested in a farm stay. Options like this are available to those wanting to relax or participate on a working farm such as rice, wheat, other crops, fruit and vegetables, beef cattle, sheep, dairy, etc.

Accommodation can be in the farmer's homestead or in private quarters. Activities available will vary but could include horse riding, feeding farm animals, swimming in rivers or pools and just relaxing and taking in the surroundings. There are a number of useful websites to visit for contact details of farm stays.

Australian Farm Stay www.australianfarmstay.com.au provides a listing of farms to contact.

Pubs and hotels

All around Australia, but mostly outside of the major cities, you can find accommodation in a good, old Aussie pub. Pubs are an integral part of Australian life, particularly in rural areas. This is why most pubs are large and very grand.

The quality can vary and is largely due to the age of the building but the novelty is the attraction. Most accommodation will be in a room with shared facilities although some rooms may have en-suites. Most of the pubs will have a dining room offering good-quality Australian meals. There will also be many locals at the bar swapping stories of the day.

Be careful when staying in pubs as some now hire bands or a DJ to bring in the trade and this may lead to noise upstairs.

The best way to find accommodation in a pub is to pop in and ask if any rooms are available. Otherwise, try a website such as:

Pubstay www.pubstay.org.au

Long-term accommodation

It is an Aussie dream to own a home. It is a traveller's dream just to find somewhere to unpack the luggage!

If you're one of the lucky ones who have a bed or even a floor to sleep on, you're off to a good start; finding rental accommodation for just a few months can be a daunting task.

There are hostels that allow long-term stays but if you can make a commitment for a few months, moving into a flat or house may be the way to go.

Renting a flat/house

Renting a flat or house requires a commitment of at least three months but in the case of backpackers/travellers it seems that nobody really wants the responsibility of having their name on a lease. If you are travelling alone, moving into an established flat or house is ideal. This way you only need to worry about paying the weekly rent and any expenses.

There is a lot of competition for decent rooms in flat and house shares, as many travellers want to get out of a hostel and spread out, which is only natural. You do have the choice of either living with other travellers or sharing with an Australian. A greater commitment is required if you're living with an Australian as they will prefer someone staying long-term. But hey, people move in and out of flats all the time, just look at the accommodation classifieds. If you are asked how long you intend staying, you can always say indefinitely. Then, if you decide to go travelling after a couple of months, that is totally up to you.

Moving into a travellers' flat can be more relaxed as they are used to people going off travelling. When you move in, sort out how the bills are paid; do you buy your own food or is there a kitty which everyone contributes to? Are there particular times for the bathroom or a roster for chores, etc.? Many travellers may be frugal and with no formal commitment to bind them can easily pack up and take off leaving bills behind.

Beware of freeloaders also. During your travels you will meet up with a lot of people and many won't say no to a free night's accommodation on your floor. Sometimes a night can increase to a few days then a week, etc. They should make some kind of contribution.

Sometimes sharing a flat or house can lead to a communal existence. If you've heard stories of 10 people living in a three-bedroom flat, believe it; these rumours are true as many travellers want cheap accommodation and this is one way to do it. You will need to be an easy-going person to live like this because you won't have much privacy, but the social life should be great.

A room in a flat or house share can be around A$150+ a week, but this does depend on a number of factors including the area and how many bedrooms there are in the accommodation. According to the (24th October 2007) the average rent for an apartment is A$380 a week in Sydney and A$290 a week in Melbourne. With two of you in a room this works out cheaper.

Setting up a flat or house

If there is a group of you, you could set up your own flat. First you have to find one and when you do, most landlords require four to eight weeks rent in advance plus a bond of usually four weeks rent. So if you find, say, a two-bedroom place at A$300 a week, it could cost up to A$3600 just to move in.

If you have never rented before there is a renting guide available from real estate agents, which explains the rights and responsibilities of tenants and landlords.

All bonds (deposits) paid in Australia must be registered with the bond board, which is a government-run board overseeing bond monies. Real estate agents can register your bond for you. The bond board holds and invests the money, so on its return you may receive some interest.

When you move out, an inspection of the flat or house is undertaken. If there is no damage, etc. the board is notified and you will receive your bond back, usually within a few days. Payment can be made in various ways such as a cash cheque or direct credit to a bank account.

Be careful of hidden extras such as fees or bonds for connecting the phone (which you will need if looking for work), electricity and gas. If you are from overseas, you may need to pay a security bond.

For connection of the above services, look in the phone book.

TIP: Most flats/houses will be rented unfurnished. Here are some tips for furnishing your new abode cheaply:
  To get cheap furniture:
  - Cheap furniture can be bought at opportunity shops like St Vincent de Paul or the Salvation Army.
  - TV, fridges and other electrical goods can be rented from shops like Rentlo www.rentlo.com.au for a certain amount per month. However, it should be noted that you will probably have to take out a lease on the rental items for at lease six months.
  - Bargain basement $2 shops are all over the place and are very good for small household items like cutlery and other kitchen stuff.

Leaving before lease is up

If you want out of your lease before the time is up, you will have to pay money for the time that the flat or house will be unoccupied. If you can find someone to take over the lease for the remaining time, such as another traveller, you can usually roll over the lease and bond. Check with your landlord, agent and the rent board about this.

Finding a flat or house share

Hostel notice boards often advertise vacancies in flats. Look in the Wednesday and Saturday city newspapers, local newspapers or visit a real estate agent. Backpackers may like to visit the Travellers Contact Point, 7th Floor, Dymocks Building, 428 George St, Sydney, Tel: 1300 855 569 or visit www.travellers.com.au.

Backpacker magazines websites have on-line noticeboards where you can place or read accommodation ads.

Most rentals are for six to 12 months, although you may find shorter leases for three months. Most properties are unfurnished but furnished properties can be found. They will cost more but will suit you better as you don't want to buy furniture. You could rent some though.

When visiting real estate agents dress neatly, as that first impression counts. If they don't like the look of you because you've come from the beach to see them, they can tell you nothing is available. I realise overseas visitors can't hide their accent, but don't mention that you are a backpacker on a working holiday as their attitude can change. I have found this especially so in Kings Cross. They often think: Another backpacker, you're a risk, and don't have the time of day for you.

So don't let them treat you like a second-class citizen. Play them at their own game and dress appropriately – maybe in your work clothes, which will show them you are employed. Produce references. They do prefer them to be Australian but if overseas ones are all you have, then so be it. Try to commit for as long as possible.

Backpacker magazine websites have noticeboards where you can place and read accommodation advertisements.

Serviced apartments

Another option is to stay in a serviced holiday flat/unit. This type of accommodation comes in fully furnished studios or one, two and three-bedroom places.

They can work out to be more expensive than renting a flat/house on a lease (possibly twice as much, even more during school holidays) but hey, you won't have a bond to pay, you won't have to connect and pay for electricity, gas and phone, the accommodation is serviced (usually weekly). They are also fully furnished including a fully equipped kitchen, TV and possibly cable. You will definitely not have to worry about not fulfilling that six-month lease commitment.

Holiday flats can be rented weekly or monthly, which means you have more control over your time. It's an option to think about. Look in the yellow pages phone book under accommodation, holiday or serviced apartments to find places. A good website to visit is www.lastminute.com.au, which lists this type of accommodation. It also provides an overview of the properties available and their price.

Between a hostel and a flat/house share

If a hostel isn't for you and you don't want to take out a lease on a flat or house and are looking for something in between then you are in luck. There are a couple of options available:

Sleeping with the Enemy is aimed at backpackers who don't want to live in a hostel and don't want to take out a lease on a property. Sleeping with the Enemy has fully furnished properties available where you can stay for a weekly rate that includes everything, all bills and unlimited internet access. They have properties in Sydney and Cairns. You can make an enquiry online at:

www.sleepingwiththeenemy.com
Tel: 1300 309 468

Another company to try (if in Sydney) that offers furnished apartments is:

Furnished Property Group www.furnishedproperty.com.au
Suite 806, Harley Place, 251 Oxford St
Bondi Junction NSW 2022
Tel: (02) 9387 7277
Email: info@furnishedproperty.com.au

House sitting

Another option that may be of interest is house sitting. As the name suggests, you will be sitting (looking after) someone's house for them during their absence. You will be expected to care for pets, keep the home clean and tidy, maintain the garden, put the bins out, etc. For doing these things you will be able to live rent-free in the fully furnished accommodation for the agreed period. If interested, you should contact **Housesitters** to register your details.

Housesitters www.housesitters.com.au
Tel: in Australia 1800 502 002
Tel: from overseas +61 2 4944 4222

Useful websites for finding accommodation

www.domain.com.au
www.flatmatefinders.com.au
www.flatmates.com.au
www.justlisted.com.au
www.lastminute.com.au
www.realestate.com.au

Living in Sydney
(for overseas working holiday makers)

Many travellers, particularly overseas working holiday makers, set up home in Sydney. Accommodation ranges from blocks of flats and units to inner-city terraces to three-bedroom fibro and brick homes.

The Sydney metropolitan area can be divided into roughly five areas: the inner-city suburbs, the eastern suburbs, the northern suburbs, the southern suburbs and the western suburbs.

Most travellers find accommodation in the inner-city suburbs around Glebe, Surry Hills and Newtown. Other popular places are Woolloomooloo, Elizabeth Bay, Bondi and Coogee, which are in the eastern suburbs. Living near a beach is a favourite option, as you can come home from a hard day's work and go for a swim or surf. Popular beach side suburbs are Bondi and Coogee in the eastern suburbs that are also close to the city for work opportunities.

The northern suburbs are often referred to as the 'silvertail suburbs' because the rich and famous favour the north shore of the harbour. Working holiday makers once again favour the beach suburbs, notably Manly, but many young Australians live near and around North Sydney as it is close to work, the public transport is good and there are loads of eateries and pubs to try.

The western suburbs are a little far out for working holiday makers as are most southern suburbs, although there are some beautiful beaches, particularly Cronulla and long-term accommodation places available.

PART III– Working in Australia

There are many work opportunities in Australia for residents and overseas working holiday makers who are seeking full-time and casual employment, which is good news. Having a variety of skills, being prepared to try new things, even without the appropriate skills, and having the desire to get out and find work, all enhance your prospects.

Employers have told me the two things that let down travellers in their quest for finding work while travelling Australia is lack of commitment and reliability. Many just work until they get some funds and then take off. This has unfortunately meant that in some professions, job-hunting travellers have a bad reputation. So please: if you take on a position, try and fulfil your commitment as future travellers are depending on you to keep work opportunities available.

In this chapter I have tried to include as many work opportunities for travellers as possible. Of course not every profession can be covered. Some of them are too specific, need registration with appropriate governing boards, possibly require overseas qualifications to be recognised, or involve sitting for tests, which can be all too time-consuming and costly. But, hey, this gives you the perfect excuse to try something completely different. Possibly fruit and vegetable picking, cooking on a prawn trawler, working as a jackaroo/jillaroo, serving in a roadhouse or working on an island resort – positions which will truly give you a taste of the Australian way of life.

I have also made this chapter very internet-friendly by including as many work-related websites as possible. They are not exhaustive as new websites are appearing daily. However, I have visited every website I mention to confirm they will provide you with relevant content. Most allow you to register your details online which are then matched with employers who are seeking staff.

When you go looking for work one of the things that lets you down is not having a contact number. A good idea is to invest in a mobile phone so you do not miss that important call to let you know you have a position.

State by state work overview

New South Wales (NSW)

Many residents and overseas travellers set up home in Sydney. Overseas working holiday makers usually call Sydney home for about three to nine months during their stay.

Work can be found all over the Sydney Metropolitan area. Most office work is found in the Central Business District that runs from Circular Quay to Central. North Sydney is also a popular office-based work area. There is another business centre at Parramatta in the western suburbs. You will find many agencies have offices in the city, North Sydney and Parramatta.

The industrial areas are found in the south and south-west of the city. Building work is available in various areas in the city and the suburbs.

There are pockets of work for office dwellers and industrialists down south in Wollongong and up north in Newcastle where the steel works are located.

Work as fruit and vegetable pickers can be obtained in various New South Wales areas. Please refer to the Fruit and Vegetable section in this chapter.

Hospitality work can be found all over the state but mostly in popular holiday areas along the coast and in the ski resorts during winter.

Queensland

Queensland is known as the 'holiday state', and there is a lot of hospitality work available along the coast, especially in areas like the Gold Coast and the Sunshine Coast and cities like Cairns, Townsville, Rockhampton and Mackay. There is also hospitality work available on many Queensland islands.

Office-based work can be found in Brisbane and the major towns just mentioned.

Outback Queensland stations might need farm hands/jackaroos/jillaroos while fishing trawlers and yacht charter companies may want deck hands. There is plenty of fruit and vegetable picking work available, especially around Bundaberg, Childers and Innisfail for most of the year.

Northern Territory

Most people prefer to holiday rather than work in the Northern Territory as towns are remote with long distances between them.

Work can be found in the Territory on outback stations and in the resorts at Ayers Rock/Uluru, Kakadu and the Kimberleys.

There is fruit and vegetable picking in two areas – Kununurra and Katherine.

Office-based work and hospitality positions can be found in Darwin and to a smaller extent Alice Springs.

South Australia

Most of South Australia is desert so there is not much work there, but you may like to try your luck at mining for opals or living in the underground town of Coober Pedy.

In Adelaide you may pick up some office support, hospitality or industrial work.

Fruit and vegetable picking is also available in the wine-growing region of the Barossa Valley. In a few years' time when you uncork a bottle of Australian wine, you can think back to those days when you carefully cut branches of grapes from their vines.

Tasmania

Most work available is fruit and vegetable picking while others secure office-based work in Hobart or Launceston or in the hospitality industry in one of the casinos.

Victoria

Victoria is known as an industrial state with agricultural work in many areas. Melbourne offers various types of employment for office workers, hospitality positions and possibly a trade position on one of the many building sites.

Work could also be found in the Victorian ski resorts during winter.

Western Australia

Western Australia is a big state and much of it is desert. However, Perth offers office positions and hospitality opportunities. Hospitality work can be found in the popular Northbridge area of Perth and along the southern coastline. You may find hospitality work also in one of the major towns like Broome.

There is agricultural work, and also work on stations in the Kimberley region.

You could also find work on a pearl lugger out of Broome or find a position in the iron ore industry.

Finding work

The various ways to find work include Employment National, newspapers, backpacker magazines, the internet, recruitment agencies, employers, professional bodies, hostels and travel brochures. Depending on where you are, door knocking and word of mouth can be successful.

Employment National

In 1998 the Australian government replaced the CES (Commonwealth Employment Service), its national employment service, with what is now known as Employment National. Basically, instead of having one government-run organisation to help job seekers, the government has out-sourced its employment service to individual providers.

If you are seeking work, you can visit www.jobsearch.gov.au where you will be able to search specific areas for positions available.

If you are interested in working in Australian harvests, this site has a guide available that you can download. This guide advises when and where the harvests are or refer to our Fruit and Vegetable Picking section.

Newspapers

Newspapers are a great source of employment. Each edition, particularly Saturday's, carries recruitment advertisements. These ads are now repeated on their websites.

There is only one national newspaper and that is **The Australian** www.theaustralian.com.au. It is also available on the weekends as **The Weekend Australian**. Every capital city has at least one major daily while some newspapers are state-wide. They include:

Adelaide and South Australia
The Advertiser www.theadvertiser.com.au

Australian Capital Territory
Canberra Times www.canberratimes.com.au

Darwin and the Northern Territory
Northern Territory Times www.ntnews.com.au

Melbourne and Victoria
The Age www.theage.com.au
Herald Sun www.heraldsun.com.au

Queensland
Courier Mail www.thecouriermail.com.au

Perth and Western Australia
The West Australian www.thewest.com.au

Sydney and NSW
Daily Telegraph www.dailytelegraph.com.au
Sydney Morning Herald www.smh.com.au

Tasmania
The Examiner www.examiner.com.au
The Mercury www.themercury.com.au (Tasmania's daily paper)

There are also many regional papers available (but there are too many to list here). These can be picked up once you are in the area.

Backpacker magazines

There are a number of magazines catering to international back-packers however, many Australian residents will also find these magazines useful as you live, work and play your way around Australia. They include travel advice and options, typical accommodation and work advice with advertised positions. You can pick up a copy at backpacker hostels and rail and bus stations. They include:

Aussie Backpacker www.aussiebackpacker.com.au
British Balls www.britishballs.com
Safari Pete www.safaripete.com
TNT Magazine www.tntdownunder.com
The Word www.thewordaustralia.com.au

The internet

I do not need to elaborate on how people around the world have embraced the internet. Everyone now has a website. I have made this travel guide as internet-friendly as possible by including many website addresses. I would recommend you use the internet as part of your job search strategy.

There are a number of general employment websites where you can log in and either search for specific jobs or leave your CV for employers to see and hopefully contact you. Most positions listed on these sites are office-based, however blue-collar positions are also advertised. They include:

www.bluecollar.com.au
www.careerone.com.au
www.jobsearch.gov.au
www.monster.com.au
www.mycareer.com.au
www.oz-jobs.com.au
www.seek.com.au

As well as these sites I have included web addresses under each specific work opportunity. You will find that most allow you to register your details and/or submit your CV online.

Recruitment agencies

Recruitment agencies were originally the way women re-entered the work force; thus the abundance of office support agencies. Employers these days have realised the potential and flexibility gained from employing experienced staff through temping, out-sourcing and contracting so now there are agencies covering a whole gamut of skilled and unskilled professions.

Unlike agencies in some countries such as the United Kingdom, which are situated on roadsides and don't mind you walking in off the street, Australian agencies are tucked away in high-rise build-ings. Even if a consultant is readily available, most will want you to make an appointment.

When you attend your appointment make sure you dress appropriately. I have waited in many agency receptions and seen consultants look prospective temps up and down. It is their belief that if you don't dress properly for them (after all, they are your employer), you will not dress properly for their much-valued cli-ents. For office-based work, dressing appropriately means a cor-porate wardrobe. For other professions such as a chef you don't have to wear your uniform, just dress neatly.

Besides dressing appropriately you should take your updated curriculum vitae (CV), which should state your name, contact details, schooling, qualifications and list your employment his-tory from the most recent position to the earliest. Your CV should be no more than 2-3 pages in length and you should also have a couple of references that can be confirmed. Yes, agencies will contact your country of origin if they feel it nec-essary. You should also be prepared to have your skills tested, e.g. a typing test or a literacy test which can take a couple of hours.

If you are a working holiday maker take your passport, as employers like to see your working holiday visa. They'll also want your tax file number so they can deduct the correct tax when you begin work, and your bank details to credit your salary.

When registering, ask about the rate you can expect to receive. Rates are usually determined by what skills you will be using on the assignment, although some agencies put you on a specific hourly rate.

Be honest and tell agencies what your skills are so that they can place you in an appropriate position. Don't let an agency bully you into accepting a position you know you can't do. Some agencies will do this just to fill the position, although most have in-house training programs to make you more marketable.

Agencies expect you to be flexible and to adapt to their clients' needs. If you find yourself in a situation you don't like, don't just get up and leave. Once I was assigned to a place where I really couldn't stand the boss so I rang the agency. We arranged for me to go home sick while the agency found someone new to fill the position. The agency never held this against me.

Try not to get involved in the politics of the place. Be courteous, punctual and appropriately dressed. A good rule of thumb is to dress up the first day, see what everyone else is wearing then blend in the next day. Do not abuse use of the telephones.

Note that many agencies send out appraisal forms for feedback on your performance. This, in turn, can lead to you being requested again.

As I mentioned, there are temporary agencies specialising in a broad spectrum of work opportunities, and I have tried to give details of as many as possible. There is no guarantee that you will obtain work through them but to give yourself the best possible chance you should register with more than one agency.

It is usually best to register early in the week, as from mid-week to the weekend salaries are paid and consultants are busy. On Thursdays and Fridays agencies ring their clients to find out their temp requirements for the following week. This is when temp contracts are renewed.

To keep your consultant up-to-date with your availability, try and ring in at least once a day, preferably early in the morning so that if a job comes in you are fresh in their minds. Keep your mobile handy.

When agencies are offering you an assignment they will go through some details with you first. They should tell you the nature of the position, the skills required, some background information on the company, the full address and how to get there if you don't know. They should advise on any dress code, how long the assignment is for and most importantly the rate you will be receiving. Once you've accepted the assignment they will send you a time sheet. If you don't have one because the assignment is only for the day, ask the client to list on their letterhead how many hours worked, the date worked and your name, and have them sign it. You may be able to download a timesheet from your agency's website.

Payment from agencies is weekly (on receipt of your signed time sheet), on a certain day determined by them.

Any agencies listed are in alphabetical order and not in order of my preference. I have chosen them as they are happy to take on travellers. They are just a sample of the agencies available.

Rates of pay mentioned are just a rough guide and were the latest at the time of publication. They can change though, so you shouldn't automatically expect to receive them.

It is advisable to confirm that any agency you contact is registered with **the Recruitment and Consulting Services Association (RCSA)** www.rcsa.com.au. This professional governing body ensures its members meet a Professional Code of Conduct. For details about these codes please visit their website.

There are a few thousand recruitment agencies in Australia with many of them registered with the RCSA. Some I have listed under the appropriate work opportunities following.

Employers

Pretty much every company and business has a website. Most of them include employment details about working for them. If there is a particular company you wish to work for, visit their website and apply online for a position.

Professional bodies

Professional bodies not only provide information about qualifications in their area of specialisation but also often provide employment opportunities available. Some will allow you to register your details online to be matched with employers seeking staff while others allow you to search for current jobs. These include:

Accounting
Institute of Chartered Accountants www.icaa.org.au
Certified Practicing Accountants www.cpaaustralia.com.au

Advertising
Advertising Federation of Australia www.afa.org.au

Biochemistry and molecular biology
Australian Society for Biochemistry and Molecular Biology
www.asbmb.org.au

Chiropractic
Chiropractors' Association of Australia www.chiropractors.asn.au

Computing and IT
Australian Computer Society www.acs.org.au

Engineering
Institution of Engineers Australia www.engineersaustralia.org.au

Law
The Law Council of Australia www.lawcouncil.asn.au
This site has links to all the state law bodies.

Library and information
Australian Library and Information Association www.alia.org.au

Media, Entertainment, Sports and Arts industries
Media, Entertainment and Arts Alliance www.alliance.org.au

Osteopathy
Australian Osteopathy Association www.osteopathic.com.au

Pharmacy
Pharmaceutical Society of Australia www.psa.org.au

Scientific research
CSIRO www.csiro.au

Science and Engineering
Association of Professional Engineers, Scientists and Managers Australia www.apesma.asn.au

Social work
Australian Association of Social Workers www.aasw.asn.au

Surveying
Institute of Surveyors www.isaust.org.au

Hostels

Hostels can be a great source of work. As well as having a notice-board where work is advertised, they require staff to run efficiently. You could find yourself working at reception, cleaning the hostel or driving the courtesy minibus to pick up other travellers from the air-port or bus station. This work is usually found by being in the right place at the right time. Therefore, become friendly with the staff already there and make it known that you are looking for work.

Hostel noticeboards are very good sources of job information as many local employers contact the hostels when they require staff. Employers who need staff quickly often approach hostels, as they know there will be travellers there eager for a day's work no matter what it is.

Hostels in agricultural areas such as Bowen and Bundaberg are always looking for backpackers to work. Some are known as 'working hostels'. This is because the hostels and fruit and veg-etable growers have joined forces. Thus the hostel provides the accommodation and the grower organises transport from the hostel to his orchard.

Advertisements on noticeboards I've seen include: cricket umpire, swimming pool attendant, lawn mower, security guard, serving beers at the races, serving pies at the Easter Show, setting up tents and manning stalls in a circus, food preparation on a crocodile farm, telemarketing, singing telegrams, leaflet drops, handyman, courier, Santa Claus, house removalist, jackaroo/jillaroo.

Travel brochures

Even though travel brochures are designed for potential visitors to a certain place, they can be a good source of work informa-tion. This is because they provide general information about a specific area, maps of these areas (including popular tourist areas), mention tours available, details of special events and provide extensive lists of accommodation. You can use this available information to your advantage.

For instance, if you were seeking to work on the Gold Coast, the brochures would include extensive accommodation listings which will not only mention how many rooms are available but what services are available. These could include a beauty salon, tennis court, swimming pool, fitness centre, retail stores, coffee shop, restaurant, business centre, etc. Therefore, if you are a beautician, fitness instructor, shop assistant, chef, etc. you could approach the resorts about a specific work opportunity. The contact details will be listed in the travel brochure.

Another example would be if you were seeking work in the ski fields. Pick up the ski brochures from travel agencies and contact the resorts directly.

Consider where you are

Considering where you are can lead to work opportunities. Instead of sitting around thinking I can't find work, think along the lines of 'I am in a particular area and this area specialises in this industry therefore I could find work related to this industry'. Some examples of what I mean are:

I am in an industrial area therefore I could find a trade position.

I am in a mining town therefore I could find a trade position. Or, as miners need to eat, I could find a hospitality position.

I am in a major city therefore I could find office support, accounting, hospitality, etc.

I am in a town servicing the farming community therefore I could find a position as a jackaroo/jillaroo or picking fruit and vegetables.

I am in a holiday resort town therefore I could find hospitality work.

I am in a major regional centre where they grow lots of fruit therefore I could find work picking and sorting fruit.

So when you find a place you like and you wish to stay a while, find out about the local industry.

Door knocking

Door knocking is another way to find work, especially waiting tables, bar work and labouring. Just put on your best clothes, summon up the courage and walk in and ask to speak to someone about employment. They can only say 'yes' or 'no'.

Word of mouth

Fellow travellers are a good source of advice on work prospects, so don't be afraid to let it be known you are looking for work. A simple question like 'Do you know of any work going? just might prove fruitful.

Tax and superannuation

That beautiful thing, tax, is always taken from your salary. You must have a tax file number in order to be taxed correctly. See our information in the Essential Stuff chapter for applying for one. Employers usually give you a month's leeway to supply them with one, after which time you will be taxed at a higher rate if you've failed to advise them of it. The following rates are for the 2008/09 tax year.

Residents

Taxable income	Tax on this income
A$0 – $6000	Nil
A$6001 – $34000	15c for each $1 over A$6000
A$34001 – $80000	A$4200 plus 30c for each $1 over A$34000
A$80001 – $180000	A$18000 plus 40c for each $1 over A$80000
A$180001 and over	A$58000 plus 45c for each $1 over A$180000

Non-residents (working holiday makers)

Taxable income	Tax on this income
A$0 – $34000	29c for each $1
A$34001 – $80000	A$9860 plus 30c for each $1 over A$34000
A$80001 – $180000	A$23660 plus 40c for each $1 over A$80000
A$180001 and over	A$63660 plus 45c for each $1 over A$180000

The tax year runs from 1 July to 30 June each year. At the end of each tax year you have until the end of October to submit a tax return. Working holiday makers must lodge a tax return either after 30 June or before they leave.

Only residents of Australia receive a tax-free threshold. Non-residents (working holiday makers) do not. The tax you owe is the tax you pay. You are not entitled to a rebate, but you might receive a tax credit which you can include in your tax return in your home country. Some accountants advise working holiday makers to tick the resident box when you're not actually a resident so you can obtain a rebate. If instead of a rebate you owe the tax department, you will have to pay. Some working holiday makers don't pay up and leave town, but the tax department has reciprocal arrangements with some countries. After a few years, when the interest has increased the amount you owe, they can trace you and demand that you pay it. If you don't, it can affect your chances of ever coming back to Australia. If you want to know more about tax laws in Australia, contact the Australian Tax Office (ATO) www.ato.gov.au.

Superannuation

It became compulsory in the late 1980s for every worker to have a superannuation fund for retirement. 'Super' as it is called, isn't taken from your salary but your employer pays an amount equal to 9% into a superannuation fund on your behalf. For casual workers you must earn over A$450 a month for this to be paid. Eligible temporary residents are now able to access their retirement savings (superannuation) upon permanent departure from Australia. For more information on accessing this money, visit the Australian Taxation Office's website at www.ato.gov.au/super and follow the links for temporary residents.

There are a number of global online tax services providing travellers with tax and superannuation refunds. They include:

www.backpackertaxfunds.com.au

www.expresstaxback.com.au, Tel: 1800 856 829

Level 6, 155 Castlereagh St, Sydney

www.taxback.com

A-Z of Jobs

Note: All recruitment agencies mentioned in this section are in alphabetical order and not in any order of preference of the author.

Accounting, Banking and Finance

Accountants, banking and financial experts are in demand in Australia. In fact, Sydney is Australia's largest financial centre with about 65 per cent of the Australian finance industry located there including the Reserve Bank, the Australian Stock Exchange and the Sydney Futures Exchange. Several international firms have chosen Sydney as their Asia Pacific base, particularly around Martin Place and in North Sydney. Melbourne's CBD is the focus of financial and insurance services with some 600 financial institutions having offices there. Melbourne is also home to the headquarters of the National Australia Bank and ANZ, two of the largest Australian banks.

Accounting work covers a range of positions including data entry operators, account clerks, bookkeepers, part-qualified accountants, qualified accountants and auditors.

These positions can be found in commercial, financial and industrial sectors throughout Australia. If you are already working in the field, you will know just how many fields you can work in. For the working traveller your best bet is to look in the capital cities, with the concentration of work being along the east coast, namely Sydney, Melbourne and Brisbane.

Overseas qualifications are recognised and you do not need to register with a governing body unless you are planning to practice full-time. To register contact:

Institute of Chartered Accountants www.icaa.org.au
Certified Practicing Accountants Society
www.cpaonline.com.au

The more qualifications and experience you have, the greater number of positions available to you. Extensive spreadsheet knowledge will increase your marketability also. If you are not familiar with the latest spreadsheet programs but you do have experience on other software packages, recruitment agencies will often cross-train you, which means they can place you in more positions benefiting not only you, but themselves and their clients.

Rates of pay vary depending on your experience and the job you are placed in. Remember that rates of pay depend on the individual agency and the skills you will be performing in the position where you are placed. The rate ranges from A$15-$40 per hour.

Banking and **Finance** professionals with experience of at least 1-2 years are in demand to fill roles as business analysts, foreign exchange officers, fund managers and administrators, lending officers, collections and leasing officers, stockbroking, etc.

Rates of pay vary depending on your experience and the job and range from A$14-$30 per hour.

Length of assignments can vary from a day to weeks or longer. Hours can be long and it is not unheard of to be still at your desk well into the evening. But this will provide you with extra dollars to live and play a little longer later on.

Work is fairly constant throughout the year, although May to August is usually busy as 30 June marks the end of Australia's financial year. Before this date companies are preparing annual accounts, and afterwards they need to balance and report. Many firms have a company year-end that falls at a different date to the official financial year-end and they often need help during that time. Another busy time is around November/December when many are tying up loose ends to go on summer holidays.

The dress code for accounting, banking and financial staff will differ from office to office. It is advisable that on your first day males should wear a suit and tie and females should wear business attire. After the first day you will have a good idea of the office dress code and you can dress accordingly.

Accounting, banking and finance positions are advertised in the backpacker press, newspapers and websites or can be found through specialist employment agencies. There are many recruitment agencies including small ones with one office and very large ones with many offices around Australia.

Useful websites:

www.careerone.com.au
www.jobaroo.com
www.mycareer.com.au
www.seek.com.au

Specialist recruitment agencies:

Hamilton James & Bruce www.hjb.com.au
Brisbane: Level 11, 100 Edward St, Tel: (07) 3223 4300
Canberra: Level 3, 39 London Cct, Tel: (02) 6160 7000
Melbourne: Level 12, 520 Collins St, Tel: (03) 8613 1300
Southport (Gold Coast): Suite 303, Ray White House,
89 Scarborough St, Tel: (07) 5532 9577
Sydney: Exchange Centre, Level 11, 20 Bridge St
Tel: (02) 8248 7000

Hays www.hays.com.au
Adelaide: Level 17, 11-19 Grenfell St, Tel: (08) 8231 0820
Brisbane: Level 17, Riverside Centre, 123 Eagle St,
Tel: (07) 3243 3011
Canberra: Level 5, 54 Marcus Clarke St, Tel: (02) 6257 6344

Darwin: Level 6, Darwin Central, 21 Knuckey St, Tel: (08) 8943 6000
Hobart: Level 8, AMP Bldg, 86 Collins St, Tel: (03) 6234 9554
Melbourne: Level 30, 360 Collins St, Tel: (03) 9604 9604
Newcastle: Level 4, 251 Wharf Rd, Tel: (02) 4925 3663
Perth: Level 12, 172 St Georges Tce, Tel: (08) 9322 5198
Southport (Gold Coast): Level 2, 12 Short St, Tel: (07) 5571 0751
Sydney: Level 11, The Chifley Tower, 2 Chifley Sq, Tel: (02) 8226 9700
Townsville: Level 3, Zurich Insurance Bldg, 75 Denham St,
Tel: (07) 4771 5100

Link Group www.linkrecruitment.com.au
Adelaide: Level 8, 115 Grenfell St, Tel: (08) 8127 9129,
Email: adelaide@linkrecruitment.com.au
Brisbane CBD: Level 6, Riverside Centre, 123 Eagle St,
Tel: (07) 3503 3400, Email: brisbane@linkrecruitment.com.au
Melbourne CBD: Level 7, 525 Collins St, Tel: (03) 8319 1111,
Email: melbourne@linkrecruitment.com.au
Sydney CBD: Level 16, 45 Clarence St, Tel: (02) 8915 7100,
Email: sydney@linkrecruitment.com.au

Michael Page International www.michaelpage.com.au
Brisbane: Level 24, 71 Eagle St, Tel: (07) 3414 6100
Melbourne: Level 19, 600 Bourke St, Tel: (03) 9607 5600
Perth: Level 4, 181 St George's Tce, Tel: (08) 9215 9500
Sydney: Level 7, 1 Margaret St, Tel: (02) 8292 2000
Robert Half www.roberthalf.com.au
Brisbane: Level 15, 333 Ann St, Tel: (07) 3039 4202,
Email: brisbanetemp@roberthalf.com.au
Perth: Level 29, 221 St Georges Tce, Tel: (08) 9214 3865,
Email: perthtemp@roberthalf.com.au
Sydney: MLC Centre, Level 45, 19 Martin Pl, Tel: (02) 9241 6255,
Email: sydneytemp@roberthalf.com.au

Robert Walters www.robertwalters.com.au
Adelaide: Level 20, 25 Grenfell St, Tel: (08) 8216 3500,
Email: adelaide@robertwalters.com.au
Brisbane: Level 27, Waterfront Place, 1 Eagle St, Tel: (07) 3032 2222,
Email: brisbane@robertwalters.com.au
Melbourne: Level 29, 360 Collins St, Tel: (03) 8628 2100,
Email: melbourne@robertwalters.com.au
Perth: Level 10, 109 St Georges Tce, Tel: (08) 9266 0900,
Email: perth@robertwalters.com.au
Sydney: Level 47, 2 Park St, Tel: (02) 8289 3100,
Email: sydney@robertwalters.com.au

Bar work

Australians love to relax, spend time with friends and have a drink. Therefore, you will find many places to work behind the bar including at pubs, night clubs, RSL clubs, trade union clubs, sporting clubs, hotels, holiday resorts, etc. Knowing how to pour a beer is essential and being able to mix cocktails will increase your potential for finding work.

Even though it is preferred you have experience it is not necessary as there will be some establishments which will be happy to 'give you a go'. Working behind the bar also means collecting glasses, cleaning ashtrays (although most establishments are smoke-free) and keeping the bar area clean.

One requirement to finding a job is to have the Responsible Service of Alcohol (RSA) Certificate, which is obtained by doing a one-day course. The course will cover topics such as the responsible service practices and strategies for serving alcohol, legal issues that affect staff and patrons, methods to minimise intoxication and understanding contents of the house policy. All these things sound quite involved when all you want to do is work behind a bar. However, these days, people are suing the licensee of public places where alcohol is served if they leave the premise under the influence and have an accident. The course takes about seven hours to complete and is available through TAFEs, night schools and some backpacker organisations such as **TCP Training** www.tcptraining.com.

Bar work is usually found by knocking on doors, through employment agencies, and by thumbing through the employment sections in newspapers and the backpacker press. Jobs can be found all over Australia, basically wherever an establishment is that serves alcohol. So you could find yourself working in a vibrant city pub or a laid-back country one.

Useful websites:

www.careerone.com.au
www.jobaroo.com
www.mycareer.com.au
www.seek.com.au

Busking

Busking can be done anywhere, although the most popular places to ply your trade include shopping malls, outside or near tourist attractions and public transport stations. You should check with the local council whether or not you are required to have a permit.

Profitable times are during the lunchtime rush and before or after business hours when people are either on their way to work or going home. You could try busking outside popular attractions on a Sunday when many families go out for the day. The Christmas season is always a good time.

As there are a lot of buskers, those who try something different like mime artists or didgeridoo players often draw more crowds than those singing with a guitar.

You might contact various resorts and pubs in holiday areas for gigs.

Call and contact centres

The call and contact centre industry in Australia has experienced phenomenal growth even with a number of companies using overseas services. This is because companies are increasingly looking for ways to 'stand out' from their competitors. To do this they rely on call centres to obtain feedback from their customers.

This, in turn, has created a demand for call centre agents, supervisors, managers and trainers with a number of skills. These include an excellent telephone manner as most of your time is spent on the phone, an outgoing personality, computer skills (mainly data entry) and the ability to listen to questions and provide the appropriate answers.

Having previous experience will stand you in good stead for temporary and permanent positions. Having knowledge of the particular industries that use call centres (insurance, banking, retail, travel, tourism and telecommunications) will also make you more marketable. However, even if you have previous experience, most companies will provide training to provide you with knowledge of their products. Positions available include:

- Customer Service (inbound, outbound or inbound/outbound)
- Sales (inbound, outbound or inbound/outbound)
- Market Research (inbound, outbound or inbound/outbound)
- Collections
- Help Desk
- Quality Assurance

Rate of pay will vary as to what position you are doing but ranges between A$13-$16 per hour plus penalities for working out of business hours and on weekends.

Positions are often advertised in the backpacker press and the major newspapers. You could also try the following employment agencies:

Command Recruitment Group www.command.com.au
Adelaide: 211A The Parade, Norwood. Tel: (08) 8332 0522
Brisbane: Level 5, 20 Wharf St. Tel: (07) 3023 8666
Perth: Level 3, 47 Havelock St. Tel: (08) 9481 1199
Sydney: Level 3, 9 Barrack St. Tel: (02) 9262 5656
Melbourne: Level 5, 20 Queen St. Tel: (03) 9621 3399

Future People www.futurepeople.com.au
Level 11, 263 Clarence St, Sydney Tel: 9252 0633,
Email: service@futurepeople.com.au

Hays Contact Centre Personnel www.hays.com.au
Adelaide: Level 17, 11-19 Grenfell St, Tel: (08) 8410 0469
Brisbane: Level 17, Riverside Centre, 123 Eagle St,
Tel: (07) 3243 3088
Canberra: Level 5, 54 Marcus Clarke St, Tel: (02) 6257 3331
Hobart: Level 8, AMP Bldg, 86 Collins St, Tel: (03) 6234 9554
Melbourne: Level 21, 360 Collins St, Tel: (03) 9604 9690
Perth: Level 12, 172 St Georges Tce, Tel: (08) 9254 4585
Sydney: Suite G02, 59 Goulburn St, Tel: (02) 9211 9569

IPA www.ipa.com.au
Adelaide: Level 10, 144 North Tce, Tel: (08) 8210 0600,
Email: radelaide@ipa.com.au
Brisbane: Level 6, 370 Queen St, Tel: (07) 3225 7500,
Email: rbrisbane@ipa.com.au

Cairns: Suite 4, 188 Mulgrave Rd, Westcourt,
Tel: (07) 4044 2666, Email: rcairns@ipa.com.au
Melbourne: Level 20, IBM Centre, 60 City Rd, Southbank,
Tel: (03) 9252 2222, Email: ipa@ipa.com.au
Perth: 44A, Level 1, Piccadilly Square West, 7 Aberdeen St,
Tel: (08) 9463 1999, Email: reastperth@ipa.com.au
Southport, Gold Coast: Suite 401, 4th Floor, 40 Nerang St,
Tel: (07) 5509 7500, Email: rsouthport@ipa.com.au
Sydney: Suite 1502, Level 15, Tower Building, Australia Square,
264-278 George St, Tel: (02) 9220 6900,
Email: rsydney@ipa.com.au

Julia Ross www.juliaross.com
Adelaide: Level 2, 80 King William St, Tel: (08) 8212 9522,
Email: adelaide@juliaross.com
Brisbane: Level 3, 247 Adelaide St, Tel: (07) 3236 2233,
Email: brisbane@juliaross.com
Canberra: Level 2, Ethos House, 28 Ainslie Pl,
Tel: (02) 6245 2600, Email: canberra@juliaross.com
Darwin: 84 Smith St, Tel: (08) 8943 1111,
Email: darwin@juliaross.com
Hobart: 162 Macquarie St, Tel: (03) 6224 9341,
Email: hobart@juliaross.com
Melbourne: Level 13, 470 Collins St, Tel: (03) 8620 8200,
Email: melbourne@juliaross.com
Perth: Level 3, 182 St Georges Tce, Tel: (08) 9486 9600,
Email: jrperth@juliaross.com
Sydney: Level 2, 14 Martin Pl, Tel: (02) 8256 0000,
Email: jobs@juliaross.com

Kelly Services www.kellyservices.com.au
Adelaide: (08) 8409 8800
Brisbane: (07) 3405 3333

Canberra: (02) 6209 1065
Darwin: (08) 8936 3030
Melbourne: (03) 9204 4242
Perth: (08) 9229 1800
Sydney: (02) 9246 6000

Quay Appointments www.quayappointments.com.au
Level 7, 200 George St, Sydney, Tel: (02) 9251 7339,
Email: quay@quayappointments.com.au

Casino positions

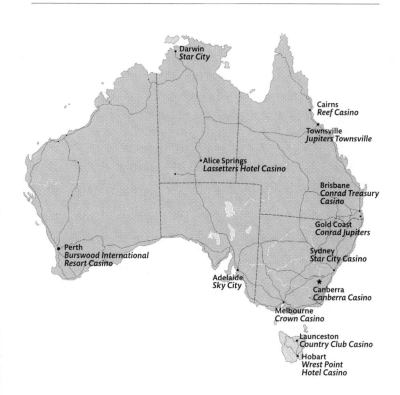

Casinos have become a major part of the entertainment industry in Australia. This is because they offer a wide range of entertainment including showcasing local and international talent and providing the opportunity to play many games. They also provide first-class accommodation, convention and meeting venues, places to relax while having a drink, nightclubs, plus a variety of eating venues.

There are a number of casinos in Australia, mostly in the major cities. This is good news if you are seeking work in this area as they all require gaming staff (dealers) for their various tables of roulette, blackjack, craps, Punto Banco, etc. and attendants for poker (slot) machines and Keno writers. It is preferred you have experience (although traineeships and training courses are available), have obtained the gaming course certificate, hold the casino operatives licence and have a clear criminal history.

To work the tables you will need to be proficient in handling chips, pushing stacks, shuffling and loading the shoe, splitting and doubling, mixed bets, multiple bets, etc.

You will need to be well groomed and neatly dressed. The casino usually supplies a uniform plus meals while on duty and sometimes free parking. As well as gaming positions there are a multitude of other positions available. Most of the casinos have resorts or hotel accommodation available which means positions in house keeping, front office, concierge and recreation centres (gymnasium instructor, lifesaver, etc) can be found. Also, casinos have restaurants, food halls and nightclubs, which mean there are positions for bar attendants, wait staff, kitchen staff and chefs, etc. Some also have convention centres and theatres.

Most casinos are open 24 hours a day and therefore you will be required to work shift work, which will earn you receive penalty rates.

For more information about casinos in Australia, you may wish to visit the **Association of Australian Casinos** at:

www.auscasinos.com. This is the site of the professional governing body of casinos in Australia.

If you are seeking a position within a casino contact one of the following.

Adelaide – **Sky City** www.skycityadelaide.com.au

Sky City is one of South Australia's largest employers. The establishment has four restaurants, a variety of bars, gaming facilities and live entertainment every night of the week. They require a variety of staff to provide services to their customers. Visit the website for current jobs available.

Alice Springs – **Lassetters Hotel Casino** www.lassetters.com.au regularly has positions vacant. If you are interested in applying for a position, send your current resume and cover letter to:

Human Resources
Lassetters Hotel Casino
PO BOX 2632
Alice Springs NT 0871
Tel: 1800 808 975
Email: hr.lhc@lasseters.com.au

Darwin – **Sky City** www.skycitydarwin.com.au

Set on 18 acres, Sky City Darwin is a beachside resort right next door to the Mindil Beach Markets. The establishment has 117 rooms, more than 503 slot machines, a VIP gaming room, TAB, Keno, three restaurants, numerous bars, a specialty coffee shop and conference facilities to accommodate up to 500 people theatre-style indoors and 2000 people banquet-style outdoors. They require a variety of staff to provide services to their customers. As many travellers come to Darwin, there is a section on their website called 'traveller's jobs'.

Sky City Darwin

Gilruth Ave, Mindil Beach, Darwin
Tel: (08) 8943 8888
Email: careers@skycitydarwin.com.au

Brisbane – **Conrad Treasury Casino** www.conrad.com.au
To access jobs available visit the 'Career' section on the website.

Cairns – **Reef Casino** www.reefcasino.com.au
You can access available jobs on the 'Employment' section on
their website or contact:
The Reef Hotel Casino
Human Resource Department
PO Box 7320
Cairns QLD 4870
Tel: (07) 4030 8876
Email: hr@reefcasino.com.au

Canberra – **Canberra Casino** www.casinocanberra.com.au
To apply for a position visit the 'Careers' section on their web-
site or contact:
The Manager of Human Resources
PO Box 262
Civic Square ACT 2608
Email: hresources@casinocanberra.com.au

Gold Coast – **Conrad Jupiters** www.jupiters.com.au
Broadbeach Island, Gold Coast QLD 4218
Tel: (07) 5592 8100
To apply for a position visit the 'Careers' section on their website.

Hobart – **Wrest Point Hotel Casino** www.wrestpoint.com.au
410 Sandy Bay Rd
Sandy Bay TAS 7005
Wrest Point Hotel Casino is one of Tasmania's largest employers.

To apply for a position visit their website and download the application form and return it to:
Email: recruitment@wrestpoint.com.au
Tel: (03) 6221 1697

Launceston – **Country Club Casino**
www.countryclubtasmania.com.au
For employment details visit the 'Employment' section on their website.

Melbourne – **Crown Casino** www.crownjobs.com.au
8 Whiteman St, Southbank VIC 3006
Crown Casino employs more than 8000 people. To see what jobs are available and to apply online visit their website.

Perth – **Burswood International Resort Casino**
www.burswood.com.au
Great Eastern Hwy, Burswood WA 6100
To apply for a position visit the 'Careers' section on their website. Here you can search for available jobs and apply online. Alternatively contact:
Tel: (08) 9362 8099
Email: jobs@burswood.com.au

Sydney – **Star City Casino** www.starcity.com.au
Located on Sydney Harbour at 80 Pyrmont St, Pyrmont, Star City is the only casino in New South Wales. It is owned and operated by Tabcorp Holdings Limited. To find out positions available visit their website and apply online.

Townsville – **Jupiters Townsville** www.townsvillecasino.com.au
Sir Leslie Thiess Dr, Townsville QLD 4810
Jupiters Townsville is owned by TabCorp and employs about 450 people. Employment information can be found on their website under the 'Careers' section.

Conservation volunteers

Conservation Volunteers Australia is Australia's largest conservation organisation. It was founded in 1982 in Ballarat, Victoria, as the Australian Trust for Conservation Volunteers but as of 1 January 2001 changed its name to Conservation Volunteers Australia.

Every year the trust involves itself with tree planting, heritage restoration, walking track construction, bush regeneration, fencing, endangered species surveys, seed collection, biodiversity protection, coastal protection, wetland revitalisation, salinity control and environmental monitoring. The trust completes about 1500 week-long projects a year. Projects are undertaken all over Australia. Examples of projects have included: reconstructing a walking trail at Cradle Mountain in Tasmania; surveying fauna in the Northern Territory desert; planting rainforest trees in the Queensland tropics; collecting seeds from native plants at Wilson's Promontory in Victoria; constructing fencing to protect sand dunes along the remote Western Australian coastline; and planting native trees on one of Sydney Harbour's islands. As you can see projects are very diverse and take place in both urban and rural areas. Current projects requiring volunteers can be found on the Conservation Volunteers Australia website.

Volunteers come from all walks of life. Not only Australians participate but also many overseas visitors lend a hand to Australia's conservation. If you have a visitor's visa, you are allowed to participate as you are volunteering your time and paying for the cost of your meals, accommodation and project-related travel (as are Australians). You can be young or old as long as you are aged between 15 and 70. If you volunteer you will be a part of a team of six to 10 people working on a particular project. You do not need experience either, as your team leader provides training. It should be noted that the work can be very labour-intensive and you will be required to work in all weather conditions. Projects can last a day or a week. However, there is a six-week 'Conservation Experience' available to international volunteers. For more details on volunteering on a project, visit the website or call the following numbers:

Conservation Volunteers Australia:
www.conservationvolunteers.com.au
Freecall within Australia: 1800 032 501
From outside Australia: +61 3 5330 2600
Email: info@conservationvolunteers.com.au

Conservation Volunteers Australia also offers positions such as team leaders on a variety of projects or as the manager running a visitor information centre. For details of positions available, visit the 'Employment' section on the website or Email:
employment@cva.org.au.

Deck hand/cook

It is possible to obtain work on a fishing vessel as a deck hand. This type of work is mostly on prawn trawlers out of Cairns and Townsville in Far North Queensland, Karumba on the Gulf of Carpentaria, Broome in Western Australia and Darwin in the Northern Territory.

Most captains prefer to take on an experienced deck hand who will be able to haul nets, sort (grade) and pack prawns (watch out for the spines) and unload the catch. Some knowledge of shipboard safety and first aid is also helpful.

Captains do take on inexperienced travellers but you must be prepared to commit to the whole season and be prepared for hard work. Many travellers go out on the boats thinking that it is a cruise in the sun. It's not.

Most deckhands are paid on a share fisherman basis and not as an employee. You sign a partnership giving you a share in the catch, which technically means you need to fork out money if a loss is made. I have been reassured that this doesn't really happen, but even so, many travellers are opting to be paid a wage instead. Check with the captain what this will be.

You can also take work as a cook on one of the trawlers. You will be responsible for buying supplies and cooking the meals, mostly breakfast and dinner with a light lunch for the crew. Cooks might also be required to help sort the prawns.

There have been stories that females are only taken on board the boats as a recreational activity. Girls should make it very clear that they will not accept this as there is nowhere to go once you're out there, and you will be sharing the sleeping quarters down below. Two female friends could go together, probably working for the one wage.

You should commit yourself for the length of time the boat is at sea or for the season. If you are susceptible to seasickness, this work might not be for you – once you've left port, there's no turning back. The length of time spent out at sea varies from a few weeks to months.

Take one set of wet weather gear, a hat, a beanie if it's cold, sunscreen and your sea legs.

To find such work you can look in the local papers, go to the pubs where the fisherman drink, go to the docks and ask the captains or leave messages on the notice boards at the wharves.

In Townsville, there are two places to look for work on a prawn trawler. You will need transport to get to them. Fisherman's Wharf at the end of Seventh Ave. At the Port Authority at the end of Seventh Ave (there is another Seventh Ave a couple of streets along), is a notice board where you can leave your details. It does say 'No Entry' to the Port Authority but the board is inside the area at the front of the building.

In Cairns, work is seasonal from March to November. Enquire at the Pig Pens, end of Tingarra St – they're called the Pig Pens because the boats are nosed in like pigs.

Some of the work is also advertised in Saturday's *Cairns Post*.

Karumba is a remote place in the Gulf of Carpentaria. There are two seasons, 1 April to mid-June, and 1 August to 1 December. Once you're out at sea, you don't come in during these times.

In Darwin, the prawn season usually runs from April to May. The time spent at sea varies.

Barra (Barramundi) boats also leave from Darwin seven months of the year; most captains make three trips out during this time. You'll find yourself working weird hours, as it depends on when the fish are biting – usually it's at night.

You can find the boats in Darwin moored at a place called Duck Pond, at the Francis Bay Dr Marina.

If you do not find a position on a boat, you could always try to find work mending nets, scrubbing the decks, etc. at the docks.

Useful websites:

www.alljobs.com.au/deckhand-list.html
www.jobaroo.com

Some companies to contact include:

Paspaley www.paspaley.com.au is a diver group of companies with its core business being pearling. They often require pearl farm deckhands to work out of their operations, which span the coastal regions from Exmouth (WA) around to the north of Darwin (NT). Contact recruitment@paspaley.com.au.

Quicksilver www.quicksilvergroup.com.au group of companies is one of Australia's leading Great Barrier Reef cruise companies. They often require deckhands to man their fleet. Forward your application to:

Quicksilver Connections Ltd
PO Box 171
Port Douglas QLD 4877
Email: reception@quicksilver-cruises.com

Sea Swift www.seaswift.com.au owns and operates an extensive fleet of vessels in Far North Queensland. They have opportunities for local deckhands to work on their fleet. To apply contact:
Email: hr@seaswift.com.au
or
HR Manager, Sea Swift Pty Ltd,
PO Box 6755
Cairns QLD 4870

Diving instructors

Imagine that your office is the clear tropical waters where you are introducing other people to the wonders of scuba diving on a coral reef. This dream can be a reality. One of the things on a traveller's agenda while travelling Australia is learning to dive, usually on the Great Barrier Reef. These people need fully qualified diving instructors to teach them in pools and in open-water sessions. While others who are already qualified will require diving instructors to look after their equipment and supervise them during their dives.

Qualifications recognised are PADI, SSI, NASDS, NAUI, BASC and AUSI. If you don't have one of these qualifications, you may need to do a conversion course. However, with one of these under your belt the world is your oyster as they say. This is because seven tenths of the world's surface is covered in water.

Positions as diving instructors can be found in many coastal areas of Australia. Some of the most popular places to dive include the **Yongala Wreck** off the coast of Townsville, the Cod Hole off the coast of Cairns and the World Heritage-listed Lord Howe Island.

Popular places for travellers to learn to dive include Jervis Bay (on the south coast of NSW), Byron Bay, the Whitsundays, Townsville and Cairns.

To find work, pick up some diving brochures and approach dive companies direct, or look in the yellow pages.

Useful websites:

www.diversjobs.com
www.flyingfishonline.com
www.jobs4divers.com
www.padi.com

Equine staff

The Australian horse industry is one of the most dynamic in the world. If you have a love of horses, some experience with them and would like to work in the equine industry then you may just find the position of your dreams as a horse handler, rider or instructor in Australia.

Overseas equine staff qualifications and professional experience within the horse industry are recognised. In some instances you do not need to be registered with an organisation/official body before you start work.

On some visas insurance is not compulsory, while on others it is, but travel insurance is strongly recommended due to the nature of the work involved in the industry. If you are coming from overseas, make sure your travel insurance covers you to work in this industry.

Positions available include; track work rider, veterinary nurse, stud groom, broodmare handler, race day strapper, yearling handler, eventing / dressage / show jumping / polo / western groom, young horse trainer, stable hand, night foaling attendant, riding instructor, trail guide and working pupil for an equestrian trainer, etc. The amount of time you have previously spent within the industry is not relevant although you must be capable of handling and tacking up a horse correctly and safely.

The wage can vary depending on your age and experience and is generally between A$560 gross per week and A$1000 gross per week. Occasionally employers supply food and accommodation, as well as other perks such as riding lessons, use of a car and petrol, etc.

Due to the nature of the industry there is the opportunity for short term and seasonal work, which suits travellers who are restricted to the amount of time they can work in one position. Many positions offer the opportunity to travel to races, competitions and sales throughout Australia, which gives people the opportunity to see Australia while they are working. The industry is continually looking for keen and enthusiastic staff.

To find a position you should use your contacts in the industry or register with a specialist employment agency such as TEP Pty Ltd, which trades as Stablemate Staff Agency. You can view their current job vacancies on their website.

TEP Pty Ltd www.tepeople.com.au
PO Box 1206
Windsor NSW 2756
Tel: (02) 4587 9770, Fax: (02) 4587 9771
Email: info@tepeople.com.au

TEP also operates an exchange program which enables Australians to travel overseas to work with horses and overseas travellers to come to Australia to work with horses. The program allows travellers to be recognised as residents for taxation purposes in Australia, which saves the traveller at least A$80 per week. Contact TEP for details.

Farm/station work – Jillaroo/Jackaroo

Those wishing to experience real outback life might want to try working on a farm or station as a jillaroo, jackaroo, tractor driver, governess or cook.

Many of these outback stations are in Queensland, the Northern Territory and the Kimberley region of Western Australia where a farm size of a million acres is not uncommon. These stations always have other staff, usually young, and often you'll find these places have their own helicopters and planes, so they may be remote but not necessarily lonely.

Work in the northern states is mostly available from March to October as during the hot, wet summer months of November to March the stations only maintain a skeleton staff. The busiest times in Western Australia are during seeding time in April/May/June, and during harvest time from mid-October to Christmas, but this does depend on the rains.

Duties will depend on the position you fill and also on what kind of farm/station it is. Stations usually run cattle, and pastoral companies farm wheat and sheep. Experience isn't always necessary but it is useful. As long as you are prepared to put in a hard day's work owners or managers of the property will often 'give you a go'. If you are worried about not having experience, you may consider doing a jackaroo/jillaroo course such as those run by the Jackaroo/Jillaroo School and the VisitOz Scheme, see details following.

A cook will obviously be cooking, usually breakfast and dinner. If the staff are working on the other side of the farm, you might need to prepare lunch for them to take along. Meals are mostly hearty, consisting of meat, meat and more meat, roasts, stews and more meat. A driver's licence is also handy for collecting your food supplies.

Jackaroos and jillaroos will be doing whatever needs doing on the farm, like rounding up stock, either on horseback for cattle or by motorbike for sheep, feeding the stock, drenching stock, mending fences, harvesting crops, etc. Tractor drivers will be preparing and harvesting crops. It is useful to have experience riding horseback or motorbikes.

Work is usually a full day of about 12 hours and the mornings start early, with the workers rising at about 5 or 6am. During the busy times you could find yourself working seven days a week.

Food and accommodation are provided and are usually very basic, either in staff quarters or possibly your own room in the main house. Your salary will be about A$450-$650 per week after tax. Most travellers are able to save quite a bit while working on farms/stations, as there is nowhere to go and nothing to spend your money on unless you go into town (which could be a few hundred kilometres away) to kick up your heels.

The clothes you should take include old jeans, long-sleeved shirts so as not to get your arms burnt, a wide-brimmed hat or baseball cap, leather gloves which keep hands warm but also have grip, gumboots for the wet weather or Blundstone boots, which are a very sturdy brand of boot, although some workers do wear training shoes. Don't forget your water bottle.

Positions are often found through remote Employment National offices. Try Alice Springs, Darwin or Mt Isa. Look in newspapers like and , and the local papers. These jobs are sometimes advertised on hostel notice boards, or you could try the following agencies:

Agworkforce www.agworkforce.com.au
Unit 1/109 Herries St
Toowoomba QLD 4350
Tel: (07) 4637 6900
Email: jobs@agworkforce.com.au

Outback International Management fills positions on outback stations in Australia, mostly in Queensland, the Northern Territory and the Kimberley area of Western Australia, and for tractor driving, machinery operation and all farm hand work in the wheat and cotton areas of NSW, Victoria and Queensland.

Outback International Management

www.outbackinternational.com.au

PO Box 1392

Rockhampton QLD 4700

Tel: (07) 4927 4300

Email: admin@outbackinternational.com

PGA Personnel recruits people for rural employment, road-houses, bars, hotels, etc. for Western Australia and the Northern Territory.

PGA Personnel www.pgaofwa.org.au

Tel: (08) 9479 4599

E-mail: pga@pgaofwa.org.au

Rural Enterprises supplies the rural sectors of Western Australia and all other states with experienced agricultural staff.

Rural Enterprises www.ruralenterprises.com.au

23A Wheatley St

Gosnells WA 6100

Tel: (08) 9398 8016

Those who would like to work on a farm or station but are worried about their lack of experience can do a course through the Jackaroo/Jillaroo School in Bingarra, near Tamworth, NSW, or the VisitOz Scheme in Springbrook, Queensland. The training programs invite people to gain a taste of outback farm or station life as a working jackaroo or jillaroo.

The programs cover such things as horseriding, yard work, mustering sheep and cattle, calf throwing, fencing and yard building, whip cracking and roping, sheep shearing, working dogs and sleeping out under the stars. They can also find you a position after you finish your course.

Jackaroo/Jillaroo School www.jjoz.com.au
Tel: 0428 617 097
Email: info@jjoz.com.au

Visitoz www.visitoz.org
Springbrook Farm
8921 Burnett Hwy
Goomeri QLD 4601
Tel: (07) 4168 6185
Email: info@visitoz.org

Useful websites:

www.jobaroo.com

Freelance travel writing

If you dream of living the romantic life of a travel writer where you are getting paid to explore the globe then read on and let us show you how.

Many magazines and newspapers rely on freelance contributions to fill their pages. Travel editors are always looking for well-written articles accompanied by photographs. If you have read the travel sections of newspapers and magazines and believe you could write something too, then you most probably can.

There are a number of opportunities available to travel writers. These include being a staff writer on a newspaper or magazine, writing travel guides and travel literature and being a presenter or researcher for a TV or radio travel program. Most of these jobs require you to have completed a degree at university or college and then it is often only luck that will allow you to work in these areas. Providing freelance travel articles and photographs to publications is another kettle of fish because you don't necessarily need to be a qualified journalist or photographer to supply articles or photos. As long as you have the necessary skills then you should be able to make money from your travel writing.

If you have been on a trip and wish to pass on your experience or tips, there are magazines and newspapers out there that would be interested. The backpacker ones especially like to print helpful hints for travellers. Those glossy magazines and newspapers on the news stands also rely on freelance contributions to enhance their travel pages.

It is necessary to supply typed text, which can be hard to do on the road. However, many travel with a laptop computer nowadays or call into an internet café to send their article/s.

If you are serious about supplying articles, research your market by obtaining copies of relevant newspapers and magazines and examine the style they use. A key to being published is sending the right type of article to the right magazine. For instance, you would not send a backpacking in the outback article to a luxury cruiseline travel magazine, you would send it to the appropriate magazines that publish backpacking in the outback articles.

There are several books that list the various markets and how to get started. These can be found in or near the reference section of most bookshops.

There are also agencies which will handle your articles and distribute them for you. They are often mentioned in the market guides referred to above, but they can take a 50% cut from any article sold.

Stock agencies will sell your photographs for you. You may find your shots in travel brochures, on postcards, on calendars or in magazines. Popular shots include photos of couples and families enjoying themselves on beaches.

You may not get rich from supplying freelance articles and photographs but it is a buzz to see your name in print. You never know you might end up with memoirs, a coffee-table picture book or a travel guide!

The author of this book Sharyn McCullum runs a correspondence/email travel writing course to help people live, work, play, travel and earn their way around the world. The course has five lessons after which students will have the skills to produce saleable articles to sell to markets. Full details of the course are available at www.liveworkplay.com.

Fruit and vegetable picking

There is extensive fruit and vegetable picking work available in Australia. The Australian Bureau of Statistics estimates about 140 000 people are employed in this industry every year. In fact, many people travel the country working the 'harvest trail', which sees them in employment all year round. This is because they know when and where the harvests are and move from one harvest to the next. You too, can join at any given time to make some money while experiencing places in Australia you may not otherwise see. Following are maps showing you where the harvests are so you can plan your fruit and vegetable picking trip.

June –July - August

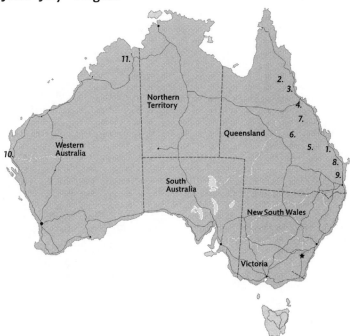

1.	Bundaberg & Childers	VEGETABLES, melons, avocados
2.	Atherton Tableland	TROPICAL FRUIT, strawberries
3.	Tully, Cardwell & Innisfail	BANANAS, pumpkins, watermelons
4.	Bowen	TOMATOES, capsicums, mangoes
5.	Gayndah & Mundubbera	CITRUS FRUIT
6.	Emerald	CITRUS FRUIT
7.	Ayr	TOMATOES, capsicums, mangoes
8.	Gympie	BEANS, other vegetables
9.	Sunshine Coast & Nambour	STRAWBERRIES, zucchinis
10.	Carnarvon	TOMATOES, capsicums, bananas
11.	Kununurra	MELONS, vegetables, bananas

September – October – November

1.	Bundaberg & Childers	VEGETABLES, melons, avocados
2.	Atherton Tableland	TROPICAL FRUIT, strawberries
3.	Tully, Cardwell & Innisfail	BANANAS, pumpkins, watermelons
4.	Bowen	TOMATOES, capsicums, mangoes
5.	Gayndah & Mundubbera	CITRUS FRUIT
6.	Emerald	CITRUS FRUIT
7.	Ayr	TOMATOES, capsicums, mangoes
8.	Gympie	BEANS, other vegetables
9.	Dimbulah	TOBACCO
10.	Stanthorpe	VEGETABLES, apples
11.	Kununurra	MELONS, vegetables, bananas
12.	Katherine	MANGOES
13.	Carnarvon	TOMATOES, capsicums, bananas
14.	Young	CHERRIES
15.	Cowra	ASPARAGUS

December – January – February

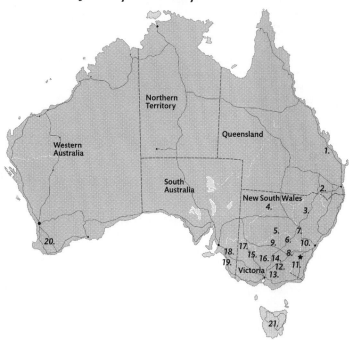

1.	Bundaberg & Childers	VEGETABLES, melons, avocados
2.	Stanthorpe	VEGETABLES, apples
3.	Moree	COTTON CHIPPING
4.	Bourke	ROCKMELONS
5.	Forbes	VEGETABLES, apples, grapes
6.	Orange	APPLES, cherries
7.	Bathurst	STONE FRUIT
8	Young	CHERRIES
9.	Griffith & Leeton	GRAPES, citrus, onions
10.	Bilpin	APPLES
11.	Batlow	APPLES
12.	Cobram	PEARS, peaches, apples

13.	Shepparton	PEARS, peaches, apples
14.	Barham	CITRUS
15.	Robinvale	GRAPES
16.	Nyah	GRAPES
17.	Mildura	GRAPES, citrus
18.	Riverland	GRAPES, citrus
19.	Adelaide Hills	APPLES
20.	Donnybrook	APPLES, vegetables
21.	Huon Valley	APPLES, cherries

March – April – May

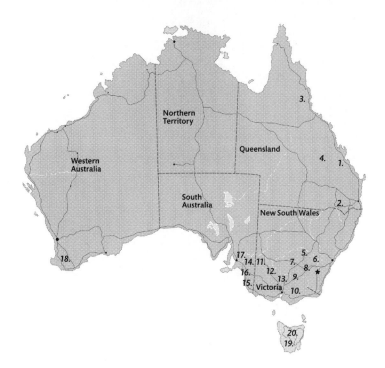

1.	Bundaberg & Childers	VEGETABLES, melons, avocados
2.	Stanthorpe	VEGETABLES, apples
3.	Tully	BANANAS, pumpkins, watermelons
4.	Gayndah-Mundubbera	CITRUS FRUIT
5.	Forbes	VEGETABLES, apples, grapes
6.	Orange	APPLES, cherries
7.	Griffith & Leeton	GRAPES, citrus, onions
8.	Batlow	APPLES
9.	Cobram	PEARS, peaches, apples

10.	Shepparton	PEARS, peaches, apples
11.	Mildura	GRAPES, citrus
12.	Robinvale	GRAPES
13.	Nyah	GRAPES
14.	Riverland	GRAPES, citrus
15.	Adelaide Hills	APPLES
16.	Barossa Valley	GRAPES
17.	Clare Valley	GRAPES
18.	Donnybrook	APPLES, vegetables
19.	Huon Valley	APPLES, cherries
20.	TamarValley & Scottsdale	APPLES, hops

What to expect

You do not need to have a qualification or previous experience to undertake fruit and vegetable picking work. For the uninitiated though, fruit and vegetable picking can be a shock to the system. It is very hard work, this is why you should have an idea of what to expect.

To ground pick or tree pick

Most harvest jobs require a reasonable level of individual physical fitness and involve regular lifting, which can be repetitious and tiring. Work can involve working from ladders or mechanical hoists, standing, kneeling or sitting while moving through the crop.

If you have never done this type of work before you might like to consider what type of crop you would prefer to pick. For instance, would you prefer climbing a ladder in fruit tree orchards to pick apples, lemons, mangoes, oranges, peaches, etc.? Or bending over picking ground crops like beans, cabbage, cucumber, eggplant, lettuce, potatoes, strawberries, zucchinis, etc? If you do not like heights or are unsteady on ladders, you may wish to choose ground crops. However, if you have a bad back, you may not like bending over all the time. If either of these options still don't appeal, then you may find work in the packing sheds grading and packing the fruit and vegetables to send off to market.

The actual picking

Farmers can request you pick their produce by either strip or selection picking.

Strip picking involves 'stripping' the plant/tree of its entire crop while selection picking will see you making the decision as to whether the fruit or vegetable should be picked. Your decision will be based on things such as colour (ripeness) and size. The second option will take place over a few weeks where you will visit the same plants/trees everyday to continue selection picking until all the fruit and/or vegetables are picked.

A tip for tree picking

If tree picking, pick the top of the tree first while your bag is light. Then you can work your way down otherwise, if you fill your picking bag while at the top of the tree, you may have difficulties getting down the ladder.

Early mornings

Many of us hate early morning starts but with fruit and vegetable picking they are a necessity. You will find that if the day is going to be a scorcher you are better off starting early in the morning anyway.

Employment conditions

Before you begin work you should find out from the grower the hours you are required to work, including the starting and finishing time each day and any house rules. If you decide you don't like the work after a few days, can you leave and be paid when you leave? Some growers only pay every fortnight and require a fortnight's notice to quit. Most importantly, find out how much you will be paid so you and the grower know where you both stand.

Payment

Payment is calculated either by an hourly rate A$10-$14 per hour, which depends on the crop, or by the bin load (piece work). The more you pick, the more you earn. Your grower will advise you.

Transport and accommodation

Your own transport is often required to get to the harvesting areas although some farms are accessible by public transport, or a lift can be arranged. In many areas now, particularly in Queensland, there are 'working hostels'. They not only provide hostel accommodation but also operate a bus service to get you to the crop on time. Some work hostels have made it difficult for pickers who find they don't like doing picking work and want to get out of town as quickly as possible. This is because they will take the passports of working holiday makers or the driver's licence of Australian residents and place them in a locked draw until your 'commitment' with the employer and accommodation has finished.

Accommodation isn't always provided, although some orchards have simple huts and an area to camp. Some of the larger orchards, especially in northern Victoria provide meals for a nominal fee or have kitchens available for use. If no accommodation is available, backpacker hostels and caravan parks are usually located in the area. Check all this out before you commit yourself to any position.

Useful equipment

Most farms are a long way from any stores so it is important you have the right picking gear with you. Otherwise your picking experience may not be as enjoyable as it could be.

As the work is outdoors you will encounter various elements, some of them harsh. You should have a wide-brimmed hat to keep the sun off your face and neck. A cap is more practical for working in trees. Most farmers are fully aware of the effects the sun can have on their pickers, which is why some will not allow you to start work without one. After all, a picker with sunstroke is no use to them. Wear sunscreen. Even in winter the Australian sun can cause sunburn quickly to those not used to spending long periods outdoors.

Or preferably cover up with long sleeves and pants – the lighter and older your clothes are the better. This is because fruit and vegetable picking can be dirty work. In particular, picking bananas can be sticky work if you get the tree sap on yourself.

Make sure you take a water bottle with you, as not all growers will supply you with a cold drink and you don't want to dehydrate in the harsh climates. It is preferable to have an insulated water bottle to keep your water cool. There is nothing worse on a hot day than drinking hot water from your water bottle. If you will be outdoors for long periods of time (which is highly likely), you may wish to invest in two water bottles. A small insulated one, which will be portable as you work your way through the crop, and a larger four-litre insulated bottle, which you can keep close by. This will then enable you to fill your portable water bottle when needed.

Depending on your accommodation and if you have a fridge available to you, you may wish to invest in an Esky to store your drink and food.

Take insect repellent to keep away flies, mozzies and other insects that hang around fruit and vegetables. These insects do not discriminate at all when they decide to annoy you. You wouldn't want to over balance and fall off your ladder while shooing flies away!

For cold weather conditions it is advisable to take thermal underwear as jumpers and coats can be cumbersome. A pair of fingerless gloves might also be useful. A raincoat or waterproof jacket will be handy in wet weather particularly in the tropical areas in the northern states, although work usually stops when it rains.

You should have your own pair of sturdy gloves – there are special ones with dimpled palms for citrus picking – and good sturdy shoes, preferably boots. Your footwear should have been worn in as new footwear could cause discomfort and distract you from your work. Spats or gaiters are useful to have. They are basically materials (nylon or cotton) which fit over your ankle and reach up to or over your calf. They will protect you from prickles and snakes that may be living in the undergrowth. If climbing ladders, it is preferable to have shoes with good grip.

Check if you need to bring any equipment such as a small knife with a curved edge for grape picking, a pair of secateurs or your own buckets. Hopefully the grower will provide these.

Your own first aid kid may also come in handy.

Most work can be found through the local Employment National service, hostels in the various areas or you may want to contact the growers directly. It is wise to ring before you arrive as the ripening time for crops can vary from those shown on the maps, due to erratic rainfall, unseasonal cold weather, drought, etc. You don't want to turn up and find that you have a couple of weeks to wait before you begin work.

There are a number of options for finding work. Many people who have done this work before usually contact growers direct as growers are often pleased to have them return. Otherwise try the following:

Useful websites:

www.fruitpicking.org – this site has useful information and you can register for current jobs.

Harvest Trail Hotline www.harvesthotlineaustralia.com.au
Ready Workforce www.readyworkforce.com.au

Employment National in association with Madec Jos Australia has a national harvest guide available. You can download a copy from their website. You can also search for fruit and vegetable picking and farm hand jobs.

www.jobsearch.gov.au/harvesttrail

Or call the **Harvest Hotline** 1800 062 332.

www.madec.edu.au

Nomads www.nomadsworld.com is known for its chain of

backpacker hostels. However, a number of the hostels, particularly in rural regions can help you find fruit picking / harvest work, as well as provide a comfy bed at the end of a hard day. The owners of the Working Hostels have set up contacts with the local labour contractors and can normally get you a job straight away. Other services including transport to and from the work-sites are available.

Hospitality

The hospitality industry in Australia accounts for one in 20 jobs, meaning around half a million people are employed on a casual, part-time and full-time basis. This is great news if you are seeking such work while travelling Australia. The other good news is it's your ability, personality and attitude that count more than anything else in finding a hospitality position.

Hospitality covers a whole gamut of professions including:

- Food preparation staff for functions and corporate boardrooms
- Bar staff in hotels, bars, cafés and nightclubs.
- Chefs – head chefs, sous chefs, chefs de partie, etc.
- Kitchen hands
- Waiters/waitresses in cafés/restaurants and hotels
- Hotel staff – front office, back office, concierge, valet, housekeeping, etc.
- Baristas
- Sommeliers (wine steward) for fine restaurants

If you are already working in this industry, you will know just how many work opportunities are available.

There is often a high turnover in staff thus people are always wanted to fill a variety of positions. Due to this high turnover plus the fact that many Australians head overseas, employers are often keen to employ travellers and overseas visitors to fill positions.

In most instances you do not need a qualification to undertake hospitality. Although it is preferred that you have experience in the field of the job you are applying for.

As mentioned under bar work, if you want to work where alcohol is served you will be required to have the Responsible Service of Alcohol (RSA) Certificate, which is obtained by doing a course. The course covers topics such as the responsible service practices and strategies for serving alcohol, legal issues that affect staff and patrons, methods to minimise intoxication and understanding contents of the house policy. All these things sound quite involved when all you want to do is work behind a bar. However, these days, people are suing the licensee of public places where alcohol is served if they leave the premise under the influence and have an accident. The course takes about seven hours to complete. There are a number of institutions that run this course including TAFEs, night schools and backpacker organisations such as Travellers Contact Point.

Compared to some countries the rates of pay are relatively high. Wait staff and bar staff can expect to earn about A$15 per hour, while chefs, depending on your level, can earn A$15 per hour plus. Australians aren't known for their tipping as it is not a requirement to do so. However, many do tip for good service so hopefully you will receive your wage plus tips on top. Hours will vary. Sometimes you may only work three hours while other shifts might be eight hours or more. You will definitely be working shift work and might find yourself working early in the morning to serve breakfast or up well into the night hours working in a bar.

Most employers will provide you with a uniform although in most cases it will be just a T-shirt. You will need to supply your own black pants/skirt and or white shirt. Comfortable shoes are a must as you will be on your feet constantly. Appearance is everything when you work in hospitality so make sure you wear clean and ironed clothes.

Although hospitality work is available throughout the year, the casual job opportunities increase from September/October until around March. This is due to the Christmas/New Year period and summer holidays when many Australians go on holidays and 'come out to play' in the warm weather.

Positions can be found all over Australia. After all, everyone has to eat and drink! However, the major cities, particularly Sydney and Melbourne, offer many opportunities. There are also many holiday centres including island resorts in Queensland, snow resorts in NSW and Victoria, and outback resorts in the Northern Territory. Details on such resorts can be found under our Resort Section further on. Queensland also offers a lot of hospitality employment from the Gold Coast up to Cairns.

Sporting venues

The major cities have sporting venues:

Sydney: SCG (Sydney Cricket Ground), ANZ Stadium (Sydney Olympic Park), Sydney Football Stadium, Rosehill Racecourse, Randwick Racecourse

Melbourne: MCG (Melbourne Cricket Ground), Telstra Dome, Olympic Park, Rod Laver Arena, Hisense Arena, Flemington Racecourse, Caulfield Racecourse, Moonee Valley Racecourse

Adelaide: Adelaide Oval, AAMI Stadium

Brisbane: The 'Gabba'

Perth: WACA, Subiaco Oval

Every year, these venues are host to events like rugby league, cricket, AFL, soccer and rugby union and they all require hospitality staff to help them run efficiently. You might want to contact the venues directly, although most of them outsource their recruitment needs.

Theme parks

Australia has a number of theme parks that require casual workers, particularly over holiday seasons. They include:

Warner Bros. Movie World, Sea World, Wet'n'Wild Water World, Paradise Country, Australian Outback Spectacular, Dreamworld and WhiteWater World.

The recruitment function at Warner Village Theme Parks (incorporating Warner Bros. Movie World, Sea World, Wet'n'Wild Water World, Paradise Country and Australian Outback Spectacular) is centralised. Therefore, you only need to submit one application to be considered at any of their theme parks.

To ensure that guests get star treatment at these theme parks a key factor to employment is your personality, enthusiasm, personal presentation, politeness, availability, friendliness, attitude, skills set and education.

Types of roles available

Show and Entertainment: Performers, Dancers, Show Technicians, Atmosphere Performers, Wardrobe Assistants, Show Announcers, Jackaroos, Jillaroos and Stunt Performers

Human Resources: Recruitment, Training and Payroll

Retail: Sales Assistants, Warehouse Attendants, Product Development, Buyers and Mobile Attendants

Accounting and Information Systems: Accounts Clerks, Cashiers, Accountants and System Administrators

Operations: Attraction Presenters and Attendants, Guest Services, Cleaning, Security and Lifeguards

Marketing: Publicity and Promotions, Advertising, Research, Sales and International Marketing

Food and Beverage: Restaurants, Fast Food, Mobile Attendants, Chefs, Kitchen Stewards and Storepersons

Technical Services: Engineering Tradespersons, Grounds Persons, Carpentry, Painters and Mechanics

Marine Sciences & Wildlife: Divers, Marine Mammal Trainers, Education Officers, Water Filtration Technicians, Stable-hands, Animal Care Staff, Sheep and Farm Tour Guides

Aviation: Helicopter Pilots and Hangar Attendants

Over the school holiday periods typical seasonal positions include:

Food & Beverage: Food & Beverage Attendants, Mobile Attendants, Storepersons, Cooks, Chefs, Kitchen Stewards, Restaurant Attendants

Retail: Sales Assistants, Mobile Attendants, Warehouse Attendants

Operations: Attraction Attendants, Front Gate Attendants, Guest Services Officers, Cleaners, Lifeguards, Car Park Attendants, Water-slide Attendants

The parks are busiest from September to January with advertising done prior to the September holidays and again in November in the local, and/or www.seek.com.au. You may send your CV and a covering letter stating the position and theme park required to:

Human Resources
Warner Village Theme Parks
Pacific Hwy
Oxenford QLD 4210
Email: hr@wvtp.com.au in Microsoft Word format only.

Alternatively, application forms may be collected from the Human Resources Department or Security office at Sea World. Resumes will be held on file for a three-month period.

Dreamworld and WhiteWater World

Positions available at Dreamworld and WhiteWater World include:
- Food & Beverage Assistants
- Ride Attendants, Slide Attendants
- Sales & Photo Sales Assistants
- Snr Photo Sales/Mini-Lab
- Games Attendants
- Suit Character/Performers
- Guest Services Hosts
- General Cleaners
- Storepersons
- Security Officers
- Cashiers
- Lifeguards

More specialised positions include, but are not limited to:
- Tiger Handlers
- Wildlife Officers
- Tradespersons
- Chefs
- Administration/Clerical roles
- Supervisory roles
- Management and specialist roles

These positions are advertised in the local *Gold Coast Bulletin*, the *Courier Mail*, www.seek.com.au and you can visit www.themeparksgoldcoast.com.au to check out opportunities.

You can also submit your CV, copies of relevant qualifications and a covering letter specifying the types of positions you are interested in by emailing: dreamworldjobs@e-market.net.au.

Useful websites:

www.careerone.com.au
www.chefnet.com.au
www.gumtree.com.au
www.jobaroo.com
www.mycareer.com.au
www.prochef.com.au
www.seek.com.au
www.starchefsjobfinder.com
www.troys.com.au

IT

The term IT (Information Technology) is used to refer to an entire industry. The definition of IT is the use of computers and software that helps to produce, manipulate, store, communicate, and/or disseminate information. The information technology umbrella is large and covers many fields.

There is demand for staff to fill positions across all IT disciplines, including:

- Business Continuity Planning
- Programming
- Project Management
- IT Sales / Pre Sales & Marketing
- Data Management
- Business Development
- Enterprise Relationship Management
- Business Analysis
- Systems Administration
- Help Desk and Technical Support
- Network / Infrastructure

Positions in the IT industry are mostly on a contract basis and vary in length, which particularly suits travellers. Most IT work is found in the capital cities, especially Sydney, and to a lesser extent in other major capital cities.

To find such employment look in the newspapers. The major ones have IT sections that are published on a particular day of the week.

Rates of pay vary and range from A$20-$150 per hour.

Many positions are advertised online.

As Australia has more than 300 IT employment agencies I would need to write another book to list them all for you. Most of them are registered with and listed on the **Australian Information Industry Association** website at www.aiia.com.au.

Useful websites:

www.careerone.com.au
www.jobaroo.com
www.mycareer.com.au
www.seek.com.au

Agencies:

Kelly Services www.kellyservices.com.au
Adelaide: (08) 8409 8800
Brisbane: (07) 3405 3333
Canberra: (02) 6209 1065
Darwin: (08) 8936 3030
Melbourne: (03) 9204 4242
Perth: (08) 9229 1800
Sydney: (02) 9246 6000

Michael Page International www.michaelpage.com.au
Brisbane: Level 24, 71 Eagle St, Tel: (07) 3414 6100
Melbourne: Level 19, 600 Bourke St, Tel: (03) 9607 5600
Perth: Level 4, 181 St George's Tce, Tel: (08) 9215 9500
Sydney: Level 7, 1 Margaret St, Tel: (02) 8292 2000

Legal

There are many opportunities to work in small and medium practices, barristers' chambers, in-house departments of major corporations and government departments as solicitors, legal counsel, paralegals, legal secretaries, word processor operators, receptionists, clerical staff, accounting staff and data entry operators.

To work as a lawyer you will need to be fully qualified. If you are coming from overseas, the work available in the legal field will be mainly as office support or as a paralegal. Overseas solicitors need to sit exams to obtain their practicing certificate in Australia and due to the time involved they usually find work as paralegals instead. Paralegals can do a variety of work from filing, chronological document sorting or document discovery to research and document management. The pay rate for paralegals is about A$25 plus per hour.

Legal secretaries and WP operators should have at least two years' experience and knowledge of a Windows package, particularly Microsoft Word and Word Perfect. Most of the positions are for regular business hours, although there are some large legal firms with 24-hour typing pools where you may obtain morning, afternoon or evening work. The rate of pay for legal secretaries and WP operators can range from A$14-$21 per hour.

If you are seeking only short-term work, the length of your employment in the legal field can vary from a day to several weeks or months.

The courts close for a two-month break in January and February but I have been advised that work is still available during this time.

Positions can be found by looking in the employment sections of major papers or by contacting a specialist employment agency. Some include:

Useful websites:

www.careerone.com.au
www.mycareer.com.au
www.seek.com.au
www.totallylegal.com.au

Agencies:

IPA Lawstaff www.ipa.com.au

Sydney: Suite 1502, Level 15, Tower Building, Australia Square, 264-278 George St, Tel: (02) 9220 6900,
Email: rsydney@ipa.com.au
Brisbane: Level 6, 370 Queen St,Tel: (07) 3225 7500,
Email: rbrisbane@ipa.com.au
Melbourne: Level 20, IBM Centre, 60 City Rd, Southbank,
Tel: (03) 9252 2200, Email: lawstaff@ipa.com.au
Adelaide: Level 10, 144 North Tce, Tel: (08) 8210 0600,
Email: radelaide@ipa.com.au
Perth: 44A, Level 1, Piccadilly Square West, 7 Aberdeen St,
Tel: (08) 9463 1999, Email: reastperth@ipa.com.au

Michael Page International www.michaelpage.com.au

Brisbane: Level 24, 71 Eagle St, Tel: (07) 3414 6100
Melbourne: Level 19, 600 Bourke St, Tel: (03) 9607 5600
Perth: Level 4, 181 St George's Tce, Tel: (08) 9215 9500
Sydney: Level 7, 1 Margaret St, Tel: (02) 8292 2000

Movie and television industry

Lights, Camera, Action – The movie and television industries in Australia are booming. This has been largely due to the fact that many major movies are now being made in Australia rather than in the United States. This is good news if you are seeking work behind and in front of the cameras.

Australia has a number of major movie studios all producing and filming work here. They include Warner Bros on the Gold Coast at Movie World and Fox Studios in Sydney. This has created a number of opportunities for people to work behind the scenes or to become a star or an extra. Your best bet to find a position is to contact the studios directly or join a casting agency.

Warner Village Theme Parks have positions for Performers, Dancers, Show Technicians, Atmosphere Performers, Wardrobe Assistants, Show Announcers, Jackaroos/Jillaroos and Stunt Performers. Contact:

Human Resources
Warner Village Theme Parks www.movieworld.com.au
Pacific Hwy
Oxenford QLD 4210
Email: hr@wvtp.com.au

So, you want to be in the movies...

The theme parks and studio's management have no involvement with the TV and film production companies that hire the studio's facilities, as such, the studios or theme parks do not employ any cast and crew.

Each production company is responsible for hiring their own staff and you would need to approach the individual production companies to enquire about possible employment. You might wish to contact the **Australian Film Commission** for a current listing of productions shooting around Australia. www.afc.gov.au.

Nannies and Au Pairs

Nannies

Positions for nannies are available to those with experience and/or a qualification. Having a warm nature and a caring attitude along with an understanding of a child's/children's needs will stand you in good stead to obtain a position.

Positions vary. Before you accept a position you should have hours, duties and salary confirmed with your employer. Flexibility will be a good attribute to have because as many nannies know a child's day is full and varied. Your responsibilities will include feeding, dressing, playing and bathing your charge/es as well as providing outings, chores and activities that will stimulate them. You may also be required to undertake household chores including laundry, shopping, light housework, running errands and preparation of meals.

Hours and days you will be required will vary from family to family. If you have a full-time position you can expect to be working 40-50 hours per week. You may find yourself working for two families on a job share basis. Most positions are live out, however live-in are available. You can expect to receive a salary of about A$550 plus per week if working full-time while the casual rates are A$15-$20 per hour plus penalties for working evenings and weekends.

Au Pairs

In some countries the main reason for being an au pair is to learn the local language. Not so in Australia, although some do think the Australian vernacular is another language!

No formal qualifications or experience are required to be an au pair, but a fondness for children and a willingness to help with household tasks like running errands, shopping, walking the dog and doing housework is essential. Also, flexibility, reliability and a sense of humour are useful.

Positions are live-in which takes care of finding employment and accommodation in the one go. You will be provided with your own room, meals and receive a small wage. Most families like someone to stay with them for three to six months and become a part of their family but shorter assignments are available which will fit in nicely with the requirements of the working holiday visa.

On average your family will prefer you to work for 25-30 hours per week, for which you will receive a salary of about A\$150-\$300 per week. Longer hours may be required, for which you will be paid extra. Sort out your hours, duties and wages before you take the position.

Anyone who wishes to work in a child-care position must now provide two or three written references, a Police Clearance and either have or be willing to undertake a first aid certificate.

To find nanny and au pair work, thumb through the employment section of major Saturday or local papers. You could also pick up a copy of parenting newspapers where specialist child-care agencies advertise their services.

Useful parenting newspapers:

Adelaide's Child www.adelaideschild.com.au
Brisbane's Child www.brisbaneschild.com.au.
Canberra's Child www.canberraschild.com.au
Melbourne's Child www.melbourneschild.com.au
Perth's Child www.perthschild.com.au
Sydney's Child www.sydneyschild.com.au
These publications can be found in libraries and kids stores.

Useful agencies:

Charlton Brown www.charltonbrownaust.com.au
Brisbane: Tel: (07) 3221 3855

Dial-an-Angel www.dial-an-angel.com.au has 11 offices around Australia. Call 1300 721 111, or one of the following offices:
ACT
Canberra: Tel: (02) 6282 7733
New South Wales
Edgecliff (Head Office): Tel: (02) 9362 4225
Lindfield: Tel: (02) 9416 7511
Penrith: Tel: (02) 4722 3355
Newcastle: Tel: (02) 4929 3065
Central Coast: Tel: (02) 4323 6688,
Wollongong: Tel: (02) 4227 2611
Queensland
Brisbane: Tel: (07) 3878 1077
Gold Coast/Sunshine Coast: Tel: (07) 5591 8891,
South Australia
Adelaide: Tel: (08) 8267 3700
Victoria
Melbourne: Tel: (03) 9593 9888
Western Australia
Perth: Tel: (08) 9364 5488

Mum's Best Friend www.mumsbestfriend.com.au
677 Old South Head Rd, Vaucluse NSW 2030
Tel: (02) 9337 5110, Email: info@mumsbestfriend.com.au

Nursing

As with many countries the nursing industry in Australia is under resourced. Therefore, if you have the right skills, you should have no problems gaining employment.

If you are coming from overseas, you will need to have your qualifications assessed. The national nursing body, which regulates the standards and processes for nursing within Australia, is the **Australian Nursing and Midwifery Council (ANMC)** www.anmc.org.au. For all electronic enquiries related to Migration Skills Assessment please email: internationalsection@anmc.org.au

Before you can seek nursing employment you must obtain registration from the state registration board of the state you wish to work in. Therefore, you must contact one of the following. Each state registration board functions under independent state legislation. However, the boards have agreed on a mutual recognition from state to state, which allows you to roll over your registration to another state. This is good news if you wish to obtain nursing work while travelling around Australia.

New South Wales (NSW) Nurses Registration Board
www.nursesreg.nsw.gov.au
Level 2, 28-36 Foveaux St
Surry Hills NSW 2010
Tel: (02) 9219 0222

Nurses Board of Victoria www.nbv.org.au
GPO Box 4932
Melbourne VIC 3001
Tel: (03) 8635 1200

Australian Capital Territory ACT Nurses Board
www.healthregboards.act.gov.au
6th Floor, FAI House, 197 London Cct,
Canberra City ACT 2900
Tel: (02) 6205 1599

Nurses Board of South Australia (SA)
www.nursesboard.sa.gov.au
200 East Tce, Adelaide SA 5000
Tel: (08) 8223 9700

Nurses Board of Northern Territory (NT)
Harbour View Plaza, Cnr McMinn & Bennett Sts
Darwin NT 0800
Tel: (08) 8999 4157

Queensland (QLD) Nursing Council www.qnc.qld.gov.au
12th Floor, 160 Mary St
Brisbane QLD 4000
Tel: (07) 3223 5111

Nursing Board of Tasmania www.nursingboard.tas.org.au
15 Princes St
Sandy Bay TAS 7005
Tel: (03) 6224 3991

Nursing Board of Western Australia www.nbwa.org.au
Level 1, 165 Adelaide Tce
East Perth WA 6892
Tel: (08) 9421 1100

Before the 1990s people became nurses by undertaking an apprenticeship style of employment with a registered health service (hospital). During the 1990s this was changed and now all nurses undertake study at either university or a college of technical and further education (TAFE) before obtaining employment in the health services.

Nurses fall into two categories in Australia: Registered Nurses (RNs) and Enrolled Nurses (ENs). Registered Nurses have attained their nursing skills by undertaking a three-year nursing course at university. Enrolled Nurses (EN) have attained their nursing skills by undertaking a one-year certificate or associated diploma courses in TAFEs. Enrolled Nurses work directly under the supervision of a registered nurse.

Once you have your registration, nursing work is available in a number of areas including in public and private hospitals, doctor's surgeries and nursing homes and with private patients. If you specialise i.e. surgical, aged care, paediatric, ICU, etc., you should be able to find employment in your field of expertise.

Rates of pay vary and will be according to the states awards. The Australian Nursing Federation (ANF) is responsible for negotiating awards covering the rates of pay and conditions for nurses. You may wish to visit their website at www.anf.org.au for more details.

Nursing positions can be found throughout Australia basically wherever there is a hospital. There are a number of specialist employment agencies that you can register with and who will find you work. Smaller agencies may only service specific areas, i.e. eastern suburbs of Melbourne and more than likely they will advertise in the local press. Larger agencies have offices in all the major cities and usually advertise in the major newspapers and backpacker press.

Following are some that will be able to help you with work in a number of areas so you can live, work and play in Australia. Most allow you to register online, however before they place you they will need to meet you so don't forget to take your qualifications and criminal clearance.

Rates of pay vary as to your qualifications, experience and the position you will be undertaking but range from A$18-$45 per hour.

There are literally hundreds of nursing employment agencies. Following is a just taste:

Australian Nursing Solutions
www.australiannursingsolutions.com.au
364 Albert St
East Melbourne VIC 3002
Tel: (03) 9419 9199
Email: allocations@australiannursingsolutions.com.au

Belmore Nurses Bureau www.belmorenursesbureau.com.au
3/47 Railway Rd
Blackburn VIC 3130
Tel: (03) 9877 2533
Email: info@belmorenursesbureau.com.au

Cairns Nursing Agency www.cairnsnursingagency.com.au
For positions in Far North Queensland and Northern Territory.
Tel: (07) 4031 0377 or use the feedback form on the website.

Centennial Nurses Agency www.centennialnurses.com.au
34 Queens Park Rd
Bondi Junction NSW 2022
Tel: (02) 9369 4325
Email: joy@centennialnurses.com.au

Clinicalone www.clinicalone.com.au
Adelaide: Level 3, 12 Pirie St
Tel: (08) 8468 8062
Brisbane: Level 4, 100 Eagle, Tel: (07) 3100 1303,
Cairns Qld: Level 1, 17 Spence St, Tel: 1300 658 899 or
(07) 4031 8755
Canberra: Level 12, 15 London Cct, Tel: (02) 6245 2930
Melbourne: Suite 3, Level 2, 19-23 Prospect St, Box Hill VIC 3128
Tel: 1300 132 190 or Tel: (03) 9946 6100
Perth: Level 7, 220 Georges Tce, Tel: (08) 9320 1633
Sydney: Level 3, 143 York St, Tel: (02) 9286 2800

Critical Care Nursing Agency www.criticalcare.com.au
Unit 19, Level 3, Edgecliff Mews
201 New South Head Rd
Edgecliff NSW 2027
Tel: 1300 687 737 or Tel: (02) 9363 5300
Email: info@criticalcare.com.au

NT Medic Pty Ltd www.ntmedic.com.au
2/3 Whitfield St
Darwin NT 0800
Tel: 1300 133 324 or (08) 8943 1555
You can also register online.

Nursing Agency Australia www.nursingagency.com.au
Within Australia Tel: 1300 300 522
Email: recruitment@nursingagency.com.au
Adelaide: 250 Glen Osmond Rd, Fullarton SA 5063
Tel: (08) 8338 1000
Brisbane: 47 Cordelia St, South Brisbane QLD 4101
Tel: (07) 3892 8000
Melbourne: Suite B, Level 1/140 Burwood Hwy, Burwood VIC 3125
Tel: (03) 9877 0555
Sydney: Floor 30, 477 Pitt St, Tel: (02) 9212 5544

Nursing Australia www.nursingaustralia.com
Nursing Australia has offices in Adelaide, Brisbane, Darwin, Gold Coast, Melbourne, Newcastle, Perth and Sydney. All offices are contactable on Tel: 13 10 95.
You can obtain the street address of the offices and email them via their website.

Oxley Group www.oxleygroup.com.au
Ground Floor, 87 Wickham Tce

Spring Hill Qld 4000
Tel: 1300 360 456 (within Australia) or (07) 3222 4850

West Australian Nursing Agency www.wana.com.au
105 Railway Rd, Subiaco WA 6008
Tel: 1300 139 366 (within Australia)
Email: mail@wana.com.au

Office support

Office support encompasses filing, clerical work, data entry, word processing and typing, as well as the work done by a telephonist, switchboard operator, receptionist, secretary, office managers, personal assistant and executive assistant. You can find such positions in a broad range of industries – entertainment, sport, financial and retail outlets to name a few.

Skills required include audio, shorthand, a typing speed of at least 50-60 words per minute and the ability to use a number of software packages. Data Entry Operators usually need keystrokes of 10000-12000 per hour. The more versatile your skills, the more positions you could be offered and the rate you receive should be higher as well.

If you don't have the skills listed above don't be put off registering with agencies; a fashion buyer friend of mine with a slow typing speed was offered work doing data entry and filing. Agencies do like you to have as many skills as possible as it makes you more marketable, but positions at a variety of levels become available, and my friend is living proof. Staff who can operate Windows packages are in real demand, particularly those with experience on Microsoft Word. An increasing number of secretarial positions require you to have a basic knowledge of spreadsheet programs, so knowledge of Excel is a real bonus, as is knowledge of

Powerpoint. and will aid your marketability. If you don't have any experience with these packages but you have used others, agencies will often provide cross training programs. This is where they will allow you to spend time in their office on their computers undertaking the tutorials to learn new packages.

The length of time you are employed in each position can vary. It is essential to stay near a phone (just keep your mobile handy) so you can take work as soon as it is offered, or else ring your agency regularly.

You can expect to receive about A$15+ per hour for data entry and about A$20+ per hour for secretarial work. Legal and medical secretaries are often required and, with a couple of years' experience under your belt, you can expect to receive a few dollars more per hour.

Corporate dress is required for most office work, although it is suggested you dress up for the first day, see what everyone else is wearing, and if the office has a more relaxed dress code then you can fit yourself out accordingly. As long as you are neat and tidy (that means ironed clothes), you should be OK.

To find office-based work, look in the Saturday papers or contact one of the agencies listed below. If in Sydney pick up copies of the free publications and or in Melbourne the where office support agencies advertise.

> **TIP:** Overseas secretaries might like to obtain a free postcode book from the Post Office, as one thing many secretaries have trouble with is the spelling of the place names in addresses – visitors' interpretations of Australian place names can cause great amusement.

IPA www.ipa.com.au
Adelaide: Level 10, 144 North Tce,
Tel: (08) 8210 0600, Email: radelaide@ipa.com.au
Brisbane: Level 6, 370 Queen St,
Tel: (07) 3225 7500, Email: rbrisbane@ipa.com.au
Southport, Gold Coast: Suite 401, 4th Floor, 40 Nerang St,
Tel: (07) 5509 7500, Email: rsouthport@ipa.com.au
Cairns, QLD: Suite 4, 188 Mulgrave Rd,
Tel: (07) 4044 2666, Email: rcairns@ipa.com.au
Melbourne: Level 20, IBM Centre, 60 City Rd, Southbank,
Tel: (03) 9252 2222, Email: ipa@ipa.com.au
Perth: 44A, Level 1, Piccadilly Square West, 7 Aberdeen St,
Tel: (08) 9463 1999, Email: reastperth@ipa.com.au
Sydney: Suite 1502, Level 15, Tower Building, Australia Square,
264-278 George St, Tel: (02) 9220 6900,
Email: rsydney@ipa.com.au

Julia Ross www.juliaross.com
Adelaide: Level 2, 80 King William St
Tel: (08) 8212 9522, Email: adelaide@juliaross.com
Brisbane: Level 3, 247 Adelaide St
Tel: (07) 3236 2233, Email: brisbane@juliaross.com
Canberra: Level 2, Ethos House, 28 Ainslie Pl
Tel: (02) 6245 2600, Email: canberra@juliaross.com
Darwin: 84 Smith St
Tel: (08) 8943 1111, Email: darwin@juliaross.com
Hobart: 162 Macquarie St
Tel: (03) 6224 9341, Email: hobart@juliaross.com
Melbourne: Level 13, 470 Collins St
Tel: (03) 8620 8200, Email: melbourne@juliaross.com
Perth: Level 3, 182 St Georges Tce
Tel: (08) 9486 9600, Email: jrperth@juliaross.com
Sydney: Level 2, 14 Martin Pl
Tel: (02) 8256 0000, Email: jobs@juliaross.com

Kelly Services www.kellyservices.com.au
Adelaide: (08) 8409 8800
Brisbane: (07) 3405 3333
Canberra: (02) 6209 1065
Darwin: (08) 8936 3030
Melbourne: (03) 9204 4242
Perth: (08) 9229 1800
Sydney: (02) 9246 6000

Link Group www.linkrecruitment.com.au
Melbourne CBD: Level 7, 525 Collins St
Tel: (03) 8319 1111, Email: melbourne@linkrecruitment.com.au
Sydney CBD: Level 16, 45 Clarence St
Tel: (02) 8915 7100, Email: sydney@linkrecruitment.com.au
Brisbane CBD: Level 6, Riverside Centre, 123 Eagle St
Tel: (07) 3503 3400, Email: brisbane@linkrecruitment.com.au
Adelaide CBD: Level 8, 115 Grenfell St
Tel: (08) 8127 9129, Email: adelaide@linkrecruitment.com.au

Quay Appointments www.quayappointments.com.au
Level 7, 200 George St, Sydney
Tel: (02) 9251 7339, Email: quay@quayappointments.com.au

Recruitment consultants

The employment climate around the world has changed over the past 15 years. Employers rely less on full-time staff and rely more on contractors and temporaries to see their operations run smoothly. In turn, they turn to recruitment agencies to find them the staff they need. This in turn has led to an explosion of employment agencies which in turn has created many employment opportunities for recruitment consultants specialising in most employment areas including general labouring, office support, IT, teaching, accounting, executives, to name a few.

To find a position look in the employment sections of major Australian newspapers particularly on a Saturday. Or you may wish to contact a specialist recruitment agency such as:

Scott Recruitment Services www.scottrecruitment.com.au
Brisbane: Suite 22, Level 8, 320 Adelaide St, Tel (07) 3220 1388
Melbourne: Suite 2 Level 6, 443 Little Collins St, Tel: (03) 9670 7720
Sydney: Suite 18 Level 488 Pitt St, Tel: (02) 9221 2700

Resort work

(Queensland islands, outback and ski centres)

There are many resorts throughout Australia ranging from reasonably priced operations to five-star luxury operations. They cater for a vast clientele including families, business people, conference delegates, honeymooners, retirees and movie stars. All of them require staff to keep them running smoothly.

Most of the work is hospitality related and includes:

- **food and beverage**: chefs, bar staff, waiting staff (including silver service), kitchen staff (dish washers, salad preparers, etc.) and fast-food service;
- **hospitality**: bartending, waiting, housekeeping, room service and bellhops;
- **office**: reception, reservations, word processing and payroll;
- **retail**: sales assistants and cashiers;

As many of the resorts are remote there are also opportunities in non-hospitality-related roles including:
- entertainers, handy persons, skilled trades people (plumbing, mechanics, carpentry, electrical, child carers, medical staff, sport instructors.

The most popular resort areas are: Queensland's islands and coast, the outback areas of Kakadu and Ayers Rock/Uluru and the ski resorts in NSW and Victoria.

It should be noted that working in a resort is not a holiday. Unfortunately, resort employers commonly remark that many who find positions in resorts often leave or lose their position within a few weeks of beginning. This is because they can and do treat their employment like they are on holiday. Therefore, if you find a position in a holiday resort, please adhere to your employment conditions and only take advantage of the free use of the resort's facilities during your time off. Fellow travellers are relying on you!

Australian Resorts

Queensland island resorts

There are many islands along the Queensland coast, most of them uninhabited. Those that have been developed as resorts offer work to the traveller.

Most resorts prefer experienced people, although inexperienced people can be employed as there is often a high turnover of staff. Personality is vital in obtaining this work, as you will be dealing with people.

High season for resort work is during the winter months when Australians who live in the colder southern states head northwards for the warmer weather. School holidays are also busy times, especially over the six-week summer/Christmas/New Year break.

Most of the work is shift work and you will be required to stay on the island until your day off. Accommodation is provided on the island but you are usually charged a rental fee. Meals are included, but you should check if this applies to all your meals or only those while you're on duty. If it's the latter, you will have to buy some of your own meals. Having your own work clothes is handy, although most resorts supply you with a uniform.

Staff are usually allowed to use guest facilities such as the gym, swimming pools, bars, etc. when they are off duty, although some of the islands provide staff facilities.

There are various ways to find work on island resorts. Look in the local papers, on hostel noticeboards and at Employment National offices particularly in Cannonvale (for the Whitsundays), Gladstone, Mackay, Bundaberg and Cairns or contact the resorts directly.

Queensland Island Resorts

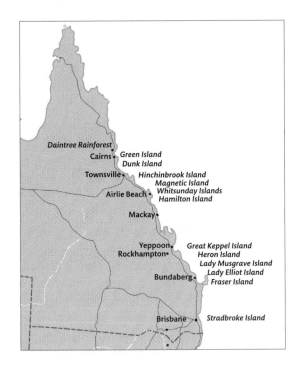

The Whitsunday Islands

The Whitsunday Islands are situated on the central Queensland coast near the towns of Airlie Beach and Mackay. The area consists of more than 70 picturesque islands with some of the islands fringing coral reefs that provide excellent diving, snorkelling and sailing. Only six of the islands have resorts on them. They are: Daydream Island, Hamilton Island, Hayman Island, Lindeman Island, Long Island and South Molle Island. The resorts vary in the degree of luxury they offer, and also in the types of positions that are required to be filled.

Some of the island resorts take care of their own recruitment. A very useful website to visit is www.workinthewhitsundays.com.au. This site lists available job opportunities in the Whitsunday area.

Daydream Island Resort. There was no specific work information on their website. Visit www.workinthewhitsundays.com.au

Hamilton Island Resort www.hamiltonisland.com.au has job information available on its website. You can search and apply for available jobs through the website. You can also call the Recruitment Centre on (07) 4948 9159 or Email hr@hamiltonisland.com.au.

Hayman Island Resort www.hayman.com.au requires staff in the following areas: watersports, marine, housekeeping, engineering, landscaping, front office, finance, sales, security, retail, medical and food & beverage. Information can be accessed from the website or Email your CV to: careers@hayman.com.au.

Lindeman Island Resort is part of the Club Med chain of resorts. The key to Club Med's success lies with its professional, international, talented and fun-loving teams, known as GOs (gentils organisateurs). Each year, thousands of GOs work in Club Med villages to create the holiday of a lifetime for their guests. Visit www.jobsclubmed.com.au for job details and to apply online for a position.

Long Island Resort www.longislandresort.com.au is part of the Ocean Hotels group. To apply for a position call (07) 4946 9400 or fax (07) 4946 9555.

South Molle Island. No employment details listed on their website. Visit www.workinthewhitsundays.com.au.

Other Queensland Island Resorts

Heron Island Resort is owned by Voyages Travel Company www.voyages.com.au. There is extensive employment information on the website including 'living and working fact sheets' that can be downloaded. You can apply for a position online. If you do not have your resume in electronic format, you can fax it to (02) 9299 2103.

Great Keppel Island Resort www.greatkeppel.com.au. There are a number of accommodation options available on the island from camping to a luxury resort. There were no employment details on their website.

Brampton Island Resort is owned by Voyages Travel Company www.voyages.com.au. There is extensive employment information on the website including 'living and working fact sheets' that can be downloaded. You can apply for a position online. If you do not have your resume in electronic format, you can fax it to (02) 9299 2103.

Orpheus Island Resort www.orpheus.com.au. There was no employment information on their website when we visited. Contact them via their email through the website.

Bedarra Island Resort is owned by Voyages Travel Company www.voyages.com.au. There is extensive employment information on the website including 'living and working fact sheets' that can be downloaded. You can apply for a position online. If you do not have your resume in electronic format, you can fax it to (02) 9299 2103.

Dunk Island Resort is owned by Voyages Travel Company www.voyages.com.au. There is extensive employment information on the website including 'living and working fact sheets' that can be downloaded. You can apply for a position online. If you do not have your resume in electronic format, you can fax it to (02) 9299 2103.

Magnetic Island www.magneticisland.com is one of the largest islands and is found off the coast of Townsville. It has a lot of accommodation available, particularly hostels and is hugely popular with backpackers.

Lizard Island Resort is owned by Voyages Travel Company www.voyages.com.au. There is extensive employment information on the website including 'living and working fact sheets' that can be downloaded. You can apply for a position online. If you do not have your resume in electronic format, you can fax it to (02) 9299 2103.

Cairns is an extremely popular holiday destination. Off the coast is **Green Island Resort** www.greenislandresort.com.au, which is owned by the Quicksilver Group of Companies. To see current jobs available visit www.quicksilvergroup.com.au. Or contact:

Green Island Resort
Administration Department
PO Box 878
Cairns QLD 4870
Email: adgir@quicksilvergroup.com.au
Tel: (07) 4052 0204, Fax: (07) 4052 1511

Daintree Rainforest

The Daintree, north of Cairns, is the oldest living rainforest on Earth. You could experience the wilderness of the area by working at the Silky Oaks Lodge which is nestled on the Mossman Gorge. Voyages Travel Company www.voyages.com.au owns Silky Oaks Lodge. There is extensive employment information on the website including 'living and working fact sheets' that can be downloaded. You can apply for a position online. If you do not have your resume in electronic format, you can fax it to (02) 9299 2103.

Outback resorts

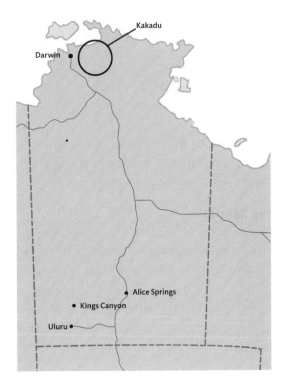

The three areas in the outback where there are resorts are Ayers Rock/Uluru, Kakadu and Kings Canyon. There is a high turnover of staff so travellers are often employed as there is no local population to draw on for employment. A 'remote' allowance is usually offered to entice staff to stay.

High season is during the school holidays and also the winter months when it is the best time to visit the outback.

The use of the resort facilities is usually allowed. Staff have to make their own entertainment because Ayers Rock/Uluru and

Kakadu are remote areas. After you've seen the main sights, what else is there to do?

Voyages Travel Company www.voyages.com.au operates the four resorts of Ayers Rock Resort, Kings Canyon Resort, Alice Springs Resort and Longitude 131°. There is extensive employment information on the website including 'living and working fact sheets' that can be downloaded. You can apply for a position online. If you do not have your resume in electronic format, you can fax it to (02) 9299 2103.

Ski resorts

When you think about Australia you might think of beautiful beaches and the never-ending outback. Now add great ski fields to the equation.

The ski resorts require many employees for efficient running during the winter season, and they are happy to not only employ Australians but visitors from overseas who have the appropriate working holiday visa.

The season

The season officially begins on the long weekend in June (the second weekend) and ends on the long weekend in October (the second weekend) but it does depend on the snow. Most of the resorts are open year-round. However, minimal staff are required once the snow melts.

The call for workers begins with advertising appearing in the Saturday employment sections of major papers (*Sydney Morning Herald*, *The Age*, *Courier Mail*, etc.) in March. The Australian national employment service 'Employment National' offices list snow job ads in their offices in April/May.

As with most ski regions it is preferred you be available to work for the whole season.

Qualifications required – general

It is preferred you have some experience in the field of employment where you are seeking a position, ie. pulling beers and mixing drinks to work in a bar, making coffee to work in a coffee shop, waiting tables to work in a restaurant, etc. Employers aren't interested in training travellers as they know you are really only there for one season. Some of the luxury resorts may not even consider you without extensive experience or a formal qualification. A friendly personality is a must.

Qualifications required – ski and snowboard instructors

Foreign ski and snowboard instructors may wish to contact the following official body about joining the organisation to allow them to use their qualification in Australia:

Australian Professional Snowsports Instructors APSI
www.apsi.net.au
Suite 11/137 High St, Wodonga VIC 3690
Tel: +61 (02) 6056 0611
Email: apsi@apsi.net.au

Many of the resorts will sponsor qualified ski and snow instructors so visit all the websites mentioned in this section for details. If possible, attend the hiring clinics held in the big resorts before the season starts.

The ski areas and employment

Australia has two main skiing areas. One in New South Wales (NSW) and the other in Victoria. There are also a couple of resorts in Tasmania but they are very small compared to the NSW and Victorian resorts.

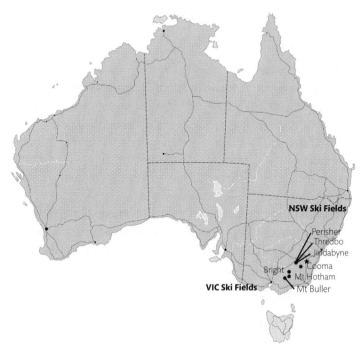

New South Wales (NSW)

In NSW the skiing areas are about 500km away from Sydney (about 4-5 hours' drive). They include:

Thredbo www.thredbo.com.au is Australia's number one year-round alpine resort. It employs about 200 people full-time and about 750 when the snow falls. International visitors who have a working holiday visa are welcome to work at Thredbo. You can browse through the 'current positions' list on their website. An employment application form can be downloaded from their website and sent to:

Personnel Department
Kosciusko Thredbo Pty Limited,
PO Box 92
Thredbo NSW 2625

Email: recruitment@thredbo.com.au
Tel: (02) 6459 4100.

Perisher Blue www.perisherblue.com.au incorporates four mountain resorts and employs about 140 permanent year-round staff. This swells to 1300 during the ski season, which is good news for those seeking work. As Perisher Blue incorporates many diverse functions, it offers a variety of positions. Your best bet to finding employment is to visit the website and peruse the 'Ski Season Jobs' then apply for a position. Perisher Blue will sponsor ski instructors. Visit the website for details.

If you miss out on a position at either Perisher Blue or Thredbo then you might be lucky in the town of **Jindabyne,** which is the largest town in the area. There are a number of places here where you can begin your job search. As well as calling into businesses randomly, there are noticeboards located at Nuggets Crossing (outside IGA supermarket) and the Butchers at the Old Town shopping centre.

Another option is to contact a recruitment agency. For all types of positions in a resort contact **Snowy Staff** www.snowstaff. com.au, Shop 34b, Nuggets Crossing, Jindabyne NSW 2627, Tel: (02) 6457 1950.

Charlotte Pass www.charlottepass.com.au is the highest resort in Australia at 1760 metres. It is snowbound for most of the ski season. There are no cars or buses, nor are there long queues for the ski lifts, which are right on your doorstep, so visitors get more time to ski and snowboard. The village is comprised of the Kosciuszko Chalet and 12 lodges holding a maximum of 607 guests. There is about 120 staff living in the village during the winter season. For details of positions visit their website.

Mt Selwyn www.selwynsnow.com.au offers visitors 12 lifts providing access to more than 45ha of skiable land enhanced by a state-of-the-art snow-making system. Employment opportunities and a downloadable application form are available on their website.

Victoria

The Victorian ski resorts are spread in a relatively wide area north-east of Melbourne around the Alpine and Mt Buffalo National Parks. They are between 160 and 400km away from Melbourne and include:

Mt Hotham www.mthotham.com.au is about a five-and-a-half-hour drive away from Melbourne or a short plane trip for those who wish to fly. It is Victoria's highest ski resort and is at the heart of the Great Alpine Road region. Along with Hotham's range of snow sports, Hotham Village has a massive array of restaurants, bars, nightclubs and accommodation options to suit a huge range of budgets. This is good news for those seeking employment in the area. Mount Hotham's Snowsports School also requires adult and children ski instructors and snowboard instructors. Employment information can be found on their website. They have a hiring clinic in June.

Falls Creek www.fallscreek.net.au is about a four-and-a-half-hour drive away from Melbourne. Falls Creek is located entirely above the snowline and cars are not permitted in the snow-filled village, so visitors either stay on the mountain or at nearby Bogong Village or Mt Beauty and travel 15 or 30 kilometres respectively to the resort each day. Employees usually live and work on the mountain, giving them an opportunity to experience resort life. For employment details visit their website.

If interested in a position as a lift operator, snow sports instructor, mechanic, snow maker, snow groomer, ticket seller, retail position, cleaner or admin staff, visit Falls Creek Ski Lifts Pty Ltd www.skifalls.com.au.

Mt Buller Alpine Resort www.mtbuller.com.au is only a three-hour drive from Melbourne making it a very popular weekend getaway. It rises to an altitude of 1805 metres above sea level and is emerging as Australia's best all-season alpine resort. There are 25 ski lifts capable of moving 40000 people every hour. The season opens in early June although snowmaking generally begins in late May. There are about 7000 beds available at the resort in hotels, commercial lodges and clubs. If you don't secure work in the resort area, a further 2300 beds are available in nearby towns such as Mansfield, about a 45-minute drive. A list of employment options is available on their website.

Mt Baw Baw www.mountbawbaw.com.au is a relatively small resort just 173km east of Melbourne (a two-and-a-half-hour drive). It is a very popular destination for day-trippers and an ideal weekend holiday for those wishing to learn to ski. As with most ski resorts there is on-mountain and off-mountain accommodation, and all the associated facilities a visitor requires including cafés, restaurants, etc. Extensive employment information can be found on the website. For more information:

Email: employment@mountbawbaw.com.au

Lake Mountain is Australia's premier cross country ski resort and very popular with families who want to introduce their children to the snow. Lake Mountain is about a two-hour drive east of Melbourne. It does not have any on-mountain accommodation and the only facility on-mountain is the ski-hire shop, making employment here limited. Marysville, the nearest town, is about a 20-minute drive away and has pubs, cafés, restaurants, ski hire and a variety of accommodation. So if interested in working near Lake Mountain, Marysville might be the place to try.

Tasmania

Tasmania's resorts include Ben Lomond, Cradle Mountain and Mt Mawson.

Useful websites

Nannies may wish to contact **Dial-an-Angel** www.dial-an-angel. com.au, which supplies many child carers to the Australian ski resorts each year.

Snowy Staff www.snowystaff.com.au is a recruitment agency for the Australian ski fields.

Ski Australia www.skiaustralia.com.au

Useful publications

You can pick up copies of and which provide information on what's happening in the ski areas and provide contact details of resorts and businesses. You could use the information in these publications to find employment.

Roadhouses

Roadhouses are basically places to fill up the petrol tank and have something to eat. They are found all over Australia and are situated as you approach town or as you leave town and, sometimes, they are town.

Food on offer ranges from fast food served over the counter to meals in sit-down restaurants. Staff are required to cook and serve these meals and sometimes someone is required to fill petrol tanks.

Most travellers who find work in a roadhouse have arrived in town, decided they liked the place and wanted to stay. Due to the remoteness of some of the roadhouses, they are a good place to save that pay packet for future travels.

Sometimes jobs are advertised in Employment National offices or in the local newspaper, but the best way is to enquire within.

Teaching

The education sector in Australia is one of the major employment areas. This is good news if you have a teaching degree and would like to find a position in a public or private school, university or TAFE/VET (Technical and Further Education/Vocational Education and Training).

In Australia, the school year begins in late January/early February and ends in early/late December. Most schools sort out their job placement for the following year from September of the previous year on. However, there are many teaching positions (term, semester, full-year and permanent) that become available throughout the year.

Most permanent teaching jobs are full-time. However, you can also get short-term teaching contracts lasting from as short as a week to a full school term. Teachers (lecturers) leave and enter the teaching services all through the year for various reasons including maternity leave, resignations, long service leave, sickness, etc. Casual/relief-teaching positions, which are great for working travellers, mean that you could be 'on call' to fill positions on a daily basis where required.

As each sector of the teaching industry has its own way and contact details for recruiting staff I have divided the following information into Government Schools, Private Schools, TAFE/VET and Universities.

Where can you teach in Australia?

Teaching positions are available across metropolitan, rural, remote and coastal areas in Australia. Australian schools vary in sizes from just a few students to hundreds of students.

How much can you earn as a teacher in Australia?

The rate of pay for teachers in Australia depends on the level of teaching experience and the type of position, and also the state/territory.

A casual teacher with three to four years' experience could earn A$220-$290 per day. Casual teachers with less experience could earn A$95-$120 per day.

Teaching qualifications and experience

Each state and territory governs its own education system. Therefore, you must meet the requirements of the education department within the state/territory you would like to work and be registered as a teacher with the relevant regulatory body. The appropriate state/territory departments follow:

Government Schools

Australia has three levels of government: federal, state and local. Education falls under state government therefore, if you are seeking employment in a government school, you are required to apply to the appropriate centralised education department in the state you wish to work. You could contact the departments mentioned below or look in the major newspapers, particularly on a Saturday, in the education employment sections.

ACT: Department of Education and Training and Teaching in Canberra www.det.act.gov.au/employment
PO Box 1584, Tuggeranong ACT 2901
Tel: (02) 6207 5111
Email: teachingincanberra@act.gov.au

NSW: Department of Education and Training
GPO Box 33, Sydney NSW 2001
Tel: (02) 9561 8000
Email: teachNSW@det.nsw.edu.au

NT: Department of Employment, Education and Training
GPO Box 4821, Darwin NT 0801
Tel: (08) 8901 4909
Email: teaching@nt.gov.au

Qld: Department of Education, Training and the Arts
PO Box 15033, City East QLD 4002
Tel: (07) 3237 0111
Email: humanresources@qed.qld.gov.au

SA: Department of Education and Children's Services
GPO Box 1152, Adelaide SA 5001
Tel: (08) 8226 1000, Freecall: 1800 088 158
Email: decsrecruitment@saugov.sa.gov.au

Tas: Department of Education
GPO Box 169, Hobart TAS 7001
Tel: 1300 135 513
Email: epool@education.tas.gov.au

Vic: Department of Education and Training
GPO Box 4367, Melbourne VIC 3001
Tel: (03) 9637 2000, Freecall: 1800 641 943
Email: schools.recruitment@edumail.vic.gov.au

WA: Department of Education and Training
151 Royal St, East Perth WA 6004
Tel: (08) 9264 4111
Email: teaching@det.wa.edu.au

Private Schools

Private Schools do not have a centralised education department like government schools. Most do their own recruiting. Therefore look in the education recruitment sections of major newspapers in the area where you would like to work.

TAFE/VET

Like government schools, employment in TAFE/VETs can be accessed through a centralised department.

Australian Capital Territory: www.decs.act.gov.au
New South Wales: www.tafensw.edu.au
Northern Territory: www.nt.gov.au
Queensland: www.tafe.net
South Australia: www.tafe.sa.edu.au
Tasmania: www.tafe.tas.edu.au
Victoria: www.otfe.vic.gov.au
Western Australia: www.training.wa.gov.au

Universities

Most Australian universities operate and recruit autonomously. They recruit in a variety of ways including the traditional method of advertising in major newspapers. In particular, in the education section of newspaper and other major newspapers.

They also post positions on their websites. Therefore, if you know which university you would like to work at, visit their website and go to the appropriate job vacancy page.

Also visit:

www.education.theage.com.au
Select Education www.select-education.com.au
Teach NSW www.teach.nsw.edu.au, Tel: 1300 300 498

Teaching English

Australia is a popular place for people to come and learn or improve their English. For those who have the internationally recognised University of Cambridge/Royal Society of Arts Courses (Cambridge/RSA) Certificate or the Trinity Certificate in Teaching English administered by Dublin's Trinity College, you could get into this lucrative market. There are opportunities to teach individuals on a one-to-one basis, or work through one of the private language schools.

English Australia (EA) www.elicos.edu.au is the national association for accredited public and private English language colleges in Australia. If you are seeking a position in an English Language school, visit this website and search for member schools where you could apply for a position.

Or you could contact:

Berlitz Australia Pty Ltd www.berlitz.com.au
40 Hunter St
Sydney NSW 2000
Tel: (02) 9230 0333
Email: pio@berlitz.com.au

International House www.international-house.org
First you need to apply directly to Recruitment Services in London Email: worldrecruit@ihworld.co.uk and they will arrange a Network Interview for you at their Cairns office.

Technical, industrial, trades and unskilled work (labouring)

- **Technical** positions include: engineers, draughtsmen, architects, computer people, inspectors, tracers, etc.
- **Industrial** positions include: store people, forklift operators, drivers, stock takers, carpenters, fitters, riggers, etc.
- **Trade** positions include: electricians, boilermakers, painters, riggers, plumbers, toolmakers, carpenters, welders, etc.
- **Unskilled** positions include: labourers, process workers, store people, dock hands, etc.

Work can be found in a range of industries including manufacturing, mining, building and construction, transportation, warehousing, etc.

When you're looking for work, make sure you bring all your trade certificates, etc. and possibly some tools, although most agencies can lend you tools. You will need steel-capped boots (if that is what's appropriate to your profession) and work clothes.

Rates of pay vary and can range from A$18-$60 per hour plus penalties.

Unskilled work is often found by word of mouth or by turning up at building sites. Look in the papers as well as the backpacker press or contact one of the following agencies that often place travellers in positions at varying levels:

Useful websites:

www.bluecollar.com.au

Agencies:

Australia Wide Personnel www.australiawide.com.au
(for engineering, manufacturing and technical positions)
241 Blackburn Rd
Mount Waverley, VIC 3149
Tel: (03) 9847 6500

Drake Industrial www.drakeintl.com.au
Tel: 13 14 48

IPA www.ipa.com.au
Adelaide: Level 10, 144 North Tce
Tel: (08) 8210 0600, Email: radelaide@ipa.com.au
Brisbane: Level 6, 370 Queen St
Tel: (07) 3225 7500, Email: rbrisbane@ipa.com.au
Cairns: Suite 4, 188 Mulgrave Rd, Westcourt 4870
Tel: (07) 4044 2666, Email: rcairns@ipa.com.au
Melbourne: Level 20, IBM Centre, 60 City Rd, Southbank 3006
Tel: (03) 9252 2222, Email: ipa@ipa.com.au
Perth: 44A, Level 1, Piccadilly Square West, 7 Aberdeen St,
Tel: (08) 9463 1999, Email: reastperth@ipa.com.au
Southport, Gold Coast: Suite 401, 4th Floor, 40 Nerang St
Tel: (07) 5509 7500, Email: rsouthport@ipa.com.au
Sydney: Suite 1502, Level 15, Tower Building, Australia Square,
264-278 George St
Tel: (02) 9220 6900, Email: rsydney@ipa.com.au

Ready Work Force www.readyworkforce.com.au has many
offices around Australia including in regional areas.
Adelaide: 200 Greenhill Rd, Eastwood, Tel: (08) 8172 7744
Brisbane: Level 13, 307 Queen St, Tel: (07) 3003 7755
Canberra: Level 1, 10 Rudd St, Tel: (02) 6230 4778

Darwin: 49 Woods St, Tel: (08) 8923 9222
Kalgoorlie: 59 Egan St, Tel: (08) 9022 7522
Melbourne: 473 Bourke St, Tel: (03) 8629 1100
Perth: Level 3, 190 St George's Tce, Tel: (08) 9217 0510
Sydney: Level 12, 2 Park St, Tel: (02) 9269 8666

Travel consultants

Australians are big travellers not only within Australia but overseas. This is reflected in the large number of travel agencies available to supply travel services to the public. This factor means travel consultants are always in demand to fill temporary and permanent positions, especially from mid-January to mid-October.

Domestic and international consultants with the universally recognised SABRE and GALILEO proficiency shouldn't have a problem finding work – although job availability does depend on the climate of the travel industry.

As the UK, Europe, Asia and Africa are popular destinations if you have local knowledge of these areas you may find positions with travel agencies specialising in these areas. However, there are a large number of travel agency chains, backpacker travel agencies, business and corporate specialists that also require staff.

Both permanent and temporary positions are available. Temporary positions can vary in length and depend on how long the employer requires you.

There are a number of specialist travel employment agencies. These include:

AA Appointments www.aaappointments.com.au
Brisbane: Level 13, 97 Creek St
Tel: (07) 3229 9600, Email: employment@aaapointments.com.au

Melbourne: Suite 104, Level 1, 167 Queen St
Tel: (03) 9670 2577, Email: recruit@aaapointments.com.au
Sydney: Suite 2, Level 8, 6 O'Connell St
Tel: (02) 9231 6377, Email: apply@aaapointments.com.au

InPlace Recruitment www.inplacerecruitment.com.au
Level 7, 191 Clarence St
Sydney NSW 2000.
Tel: 1300 467 522
Email: enquiries@inplacerecruitment.com.au

WWOOF (Willing Workers on Organic Farms)

If you'd like to experience life working on an organic farm, you could WWOOF your way around the country. No, no, you don't have to do dog impressions, even though you will find yourself digging in the dirt. WWOOF stands for Willing Workers on Organic Farms and is an exchange program.

In exchange for your willingness to work, you'll receive food, somewhere to sleep, first-hand knowledge of agricultural methods and experience your host's way of life.

In Australia there are about 1500 participating farms. They are listed in a booklet available from the organisation listed below.

The full range of vegetable, fruit, dairy, pasture and arable farms are covered. They range from self-sufficient holdings through to fully commercial operations. Your duties on the farms will therefore vary depending on where you decide to work. Four to six hours work per day is generally expected.

Bookings from overseas should be made by mail, but once you're in Australia it is acceptable to contact host families by phone. More details about contacting your host are available in the WWOOF Australia handbook.

The minimum length of stay is two nights with an average stay lasting about six or seven days, although you can arrange longer stays with your host.

WWOOF membership is per person or per couple and includes your Aussie Farm List and basic insurance to cover you while you're working on the farms. It costs A$45 per single or A$50 per couple and can be sent via an international bank draft to:

WWOOF (Willing Workers on Organic Farms)
www.wwoof.com.au
2166 Gelantipy Rd,
W Tree via Buchan, VIC 3885
Tel: (03) 5155 0218, Fax: (03) 5155 0342
Email: wwoof@wwoof.com.au

Yachts and seafaring craft

Fancy spending your time island-hopping on the Great Barrier Reef or cruising on a steamship along the Murray? Then there are opportunities for you to spend your time working on the water. There are basically three options open to you: delivering a yacht or motor cruiser; catching a lift or finding a position as a crew member.

Delivering a yacht or motor cruiser

Sometimes people prefer to arrive at their destination by quicker means yet still have their yacht or motor cruisers available to them on their arrival. Others who have bought a new vessel require it to be delivered to them. This is why crew are required to deliver a yacht or motor cruiser to its destination. There are therefore opportunities available to work on these vessels.

Catching a lift

Wherever there is open water you will find some kind of yacht. The best way to find a lift is to frequent yacht clubs where yachts are moored and speak to the captains. Before you board, keep in mind that while, for you, a yacht may be just a means to get from A to B, for some yachties it is home, so make sure you first seek 'permission to board'.

You may like to place an advertisement on a yacht club's or sailing school's noticeboard stating that you are looking for a lift. Include where you would like to go and when. And don't forget a contact number.

Depending on the captain, you may find you either have to contribute to the running expenses of the yacht (including food) for the length of the trip (usually worked out per day), or you may be able to work your passage. Some people have saved thousands of dollars in travel costs by working their passage. Do note you may be required to pay a bond and you should find out about insurance for any mishaps at sea.

Finding a position

There are many who 'drop out' and like to spend their time in exotic locations. Some either own their own yachts or charter them. Depending on the size of the vessel, there can be positions onboard. These include: captains, mates, engineers, chefs, cooks and stewards/stewardesses.

Work can also be found during times in 'dry dock', cleaning and scrubbing hulls, painting, re-firing, mending sails, etc.

Besides speaking to captains and leaving advertisements on noticeboards (see 'Catching a lift', previously), positions can be found by contacting a recruitment agency.

There are a number of agencies that can link crew (from novices to professionals) with captains/owners of boats who require staff or a boat to be delivered.

Useful websites

www.boatingoz.com.au
www.flyingfishonline.com

Useful agencies

Australian Yacht Crew www.ayc.com.au
Email: info@ayc.com.au

Charter Yachts Australia www.charteryachtsaustralia.com.au
Shop 10, Abel Point Marina
Airlie Beach QLD 4802
Tel: 1800 639 520

Crewseekers www.crewseekers.net

Find a Crew www.findacrew.net
PO Box 1210, Mooloolaba QLD 4557
Tel: (07) 5412 1416
Email: sailaway@findacrew.net

Marine Crew Australia www.crewaustralia.com.au
PO Box 1024, Airlie Beach QLD 4802
Tel: (07) 4948 1958
Email: info@crewaustralia.com.au

Yacht Crew Australia www.yachtcrewaustralia.com
Sanctuary Cove Marine
PO Box 428
Masthead Way QLD 4212
Email: info@yachtcrewaustralia.com

The Whitsunday Islands is a very popular cruising yacht destination with a number of companies eager to hire you a yacht. These include:

Sunsail which operates from Hamilton Island
Whitsunday Rent a Yacht from Shute Harbour
Queensland Yacht Charters from Airlie Beach.

PART IV – Playing in Australia

Australia is a very large island with vastly varied terrain and weather patterns. It offers travellers many opportunities to discover just how diverse it is. This chapter has three sections: sightseeing, travel options and travelling safe, well and alone. Sightseeing will provide information on what there is to see and do in Australia. The travel options will fill you in on the variety of options you have available to travel the country while travelling safe, well and alone will provide information on travelling safe, well and alone.

Sightseeing Australia

The coach left Alice Springs on time at 8.30pm but soon the traveller sitting next to me enquired whether I knew how much longer it was until we'd be there? Her jaw dropped to the floor when I told her we weren't due in Darwin until 3.30pm tomorrow afternoon. She looked at her watch and counted around its face. 'But that's another 17 hours!' she exclaimed. 'I know' I responded. All up, the trip from Alice Springs to Darwin took 19 hours. Nineteen very long hours!

As I recovered from my trip by the hostel's pool, another girl joined me and soon revealed that she had just arrived in Darwin after a 33-hour bus journey from Cairns. But that was nothing, a guy who joined us decided against spending three-and-a-half hours on a plane to fly from Perth to Darwin and spent 56 hours on the bus. And so the stories continue of many travellers who don't realise the distances involved in travelling Australia, particularly by road.

If your aim is really to experience Australia by seeing all there is to see and experiencing all the activities there are to try, then you really need to spend as long as possible travelling. Three to six months is the norm for working holiday makers, although it really is up to you. Some people travel for years. You should take into account actual travelling time to places (and recovery time) when planning your trip/s.

To help you make the most of your trip, following is a map of major attractions including the activities available there and how long they take. Once you have a rough time-frame you can work out how to get around by linking the available options. Read on.

Some example distances in kilometres

You can roughly work out in hours how long it will take to drive. If on average you drive 100km per hour then for example, Perth to Sydney is 4057km therefore, it can take around 41 hours to drive – that doesn't include breaks.

Adelaide (SA)

1540 **Alice Springs (NT)**										
2103	3111 **Brisbane (Qld)**									
5170	2630	4712 **Broome (WA)**								
3545	2370	1703	4020 **Cairns (Qld)**							
1198	2638	1347	5518	3050 **Canberra (ACT)**						
2947	1407	3489	1865	2845	4295	3854 **Darwin (NT)**				
2626	1086	3168	1544	2524	3895	3533	321 **Katherine (NT)**			
741	2181	1702	5649	3116	670	4125	3836	3373 **Melbourne (Vic)**		
2770	3535	4492	2248	5905	3798	6914	4113	3792	3472 **Perth (WA)**	
1394	2766	1019	5502	2722	328	3731	3967	3563	998	4057 **Sydney (NSW)**

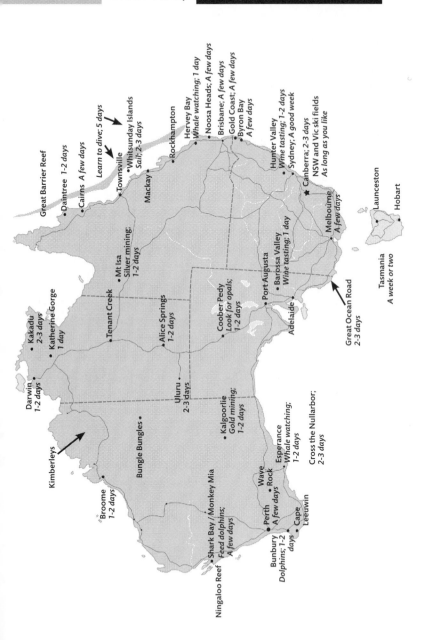

Great Barrier Reef

Daintree 1-2 days

Cairns A few days

Learn to dive; 5 days

Townsville

Whitsunday Islands
Sail; 2-3 days

Mackay

Rockhampton

Hervey Bay
Whale watching; 1 day

Noosa Heads; A few days

Brisbane; A few days

Gold Coast; A few days

Byron Bay
A few days

Hunter Valley
Wine tasting; 1-2 days

Sydney; A good week

NSW and Vic ski fields
As long as you like

Canberra; 2-3 days

Melbourne
A few days

Launceston

Hobart

Tasmania
A week or two

Great Ocean Road
2-3 days

Mt Isa
Silver mining;
1-2 days

Port Augusta

Barossa Valley
Wine tasting; 1 day

Adelaide

Coober Pedy
Look for opals;
1-2 days

Alice Springs
1-2 days

Tenant Creek

Kakadu
2-3 days

Katherine Gorge
1 day

Darwin
1-2 days

Kimberleys

Uluru
2-3 days

Kalgoorlie
Gold mining;
1-2 days

Esperance
Whale watching;
1-2 days

Cross the Nullarbor;
2-3 days

Bungle Bungles

Wave
Rock

Broome
1-2 days

Shark Bay / Monkey Mia
Feed dolphins;
A few days

Perth
A few days

Cape
Leeuwin

Bunbury
Dolphins; 1-2
days

Ningaloo Reef

Sightseeing

Sightseeing Sydney

Everyone spends time in Sydney where there is plenty to see and do, and extensive transport systems (buses, trains and ferries) to help you see and do it all.

If you want to hit the tourist trail but don't feel too energetic, then catch the red **Explorer Bus** www.sydneybuses.com.au which is the hop-on hop-off bus visiting 27 of Sydney's most famous attractions including the Opera House, Royal Botanic Gardens, Mrs Macquarie's Chair, Kings Cross, The Rocks, Darling Harbour and a lot more, including travelling across the Sydney Harbour Bridge.

You can pick up the bus at any stop along its route and then hop on and off as you please. Buses operate at 20 minute intervals making this an easy and enjoyable way to see the city of Sydney.

There is also the blue **Bondi Explorer** stopping at 19 of Sydney's picturesque harbour locations and surf beaches. The full 30km circuit takes you through Sydney's affluent Eastern Suburbs including stops at cosmopolitan Double Bay, Watson's Bay and the famous Bondi Beach. You can sit back, listen to the commentary and enjoy the rugged coastline and golden sands of Bondi, Tamarama, Bronte and Coogee beaches.

Other ways to travel around Sydney are by train www.cityrail.info, ferry www.sydneyferries.info, monorail www.metromonorail.com.au or tram (light rail).

Everyone heads to Circular Quay first to see the Harbour Bridge and the Opera House.

Walking map of Sydney –
The Rocks to Mrs Macquarie's Chair

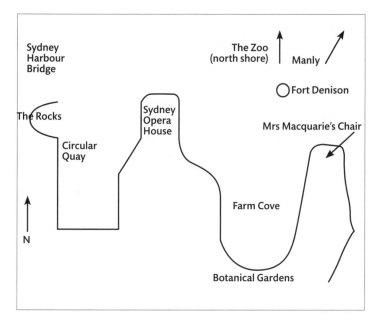

Starting at Circular Quay, where you will find many ferries servicing Sydney Harbour, follow **Writers' Walk** to **Bennelong Point** where you will find the World Heritage-listed Sydney **Opera House** www.sydneyoperahouse.com. Here you could take a tour of the various theatres and halls and walk around the unusual building itself. Maybe have a meal in one of its cafés or restaurants or see a show.

What is that castle-like building sitting in the middle of the harbour? It is **Fort Denison**, once used as a penal site and defensive facility. Its tower is one of just two surviving Martello Towers in the Southern Hemisphere. The Fort gun is fired every day at one o'clock.

Captain Cook Cruises www.captaincook.com.au, Tel: (02) 9206 1111, operate Fort Denison Ferries enabling you to visit the island. Tickets can be purchased at Circular Quay.

Leaving the Opera House, walk along the foreshore of Farm Cove – the original farming ground of the first white settlers and now the Botanic Gardens – to **Mrs Macquarie's Chair**. There you can sit back and relax just like Mrs Macquarie did in the 1800s, but you will have a view of the Opera House and the Harbour Bridge.

From here walk back through the **Botanic Gardens,** an oasis of 30ha in the heart of the city, to Circular Quay and follow Writers' Walk to **The Rocks**. This is where the original settlement of Sydney began under Captain Arthur Phillip. You can stroll along narrow, cobbled streets and among sandstone buildings that were once warehouses, sailors' homes and dens of iniquity but are now fine restaurants, cafés, one-of-a-kind shops and galleries.

From The Rocks you can ascend the pylons of the **Sydney Harbour Bridge**. Access is by the pedestrian walk-way off Cumberland Street. You might like to walk the 'Coathanger' or catch a train or bus across and take in the view. You may wish to spend 3.5 hours climbing the bridge for a bird's-eye view of the city, but make sure you book ahead through Sydney Harbour Bridge Climb www.bridgeclimb.com.

Your feet may be aching by now, I know mine were way back at the Botanic Gardens, so enough sightseeing for today.

Other things to do include:

- Take a ferry from Circular Quay to **Taronga Park Zoo** www.taronga.org.au and get the animals-eye view of the harbour. It will take a good day here to really appreciate all the zoo has to offer.
- Take the half-hour ferry ride from Circular Quay to **Manly** and visit Oceanworld Manly www.oceanworld.com.au, or stroll the

esplanade and take in the beachside atmosphere. From Manly you might want to head north to visit other beaches including Palm Beach, where some of the scenes of are filmed. Or you could walk from the wharf to the Quarantine Station at North Head.

- Still on the harbour, you might like to take a morning, after-noon or dinner cruise. These can be arranged from Circular Quay.

- Perhaps visit the **Sydney Aquarium** www.sydneyaquarium. com.au with its comprehensive collection of aquatic life in-cluding some 650 species, which are housed in a number of oceanariums.

- Take in a show at the **Entertainment Centre** or walk through the **Chinese Gardens** on your way to **China Town**.

- Sports enthusiasts might want to visit the **SCG (Sydney Cricket Ground)** and **the Football Stadium**, or get tickets to a sporting match.

- Catch the lift up **Sydney Tower**, www.sydneytower.com.au, Sydney's tallest building, to the observation level for a 360-de-gree view of the city. Splurge on a meal at one of the revolving restaurants. Choose a clear day or evening. Or why not take the Skywalk, a unique exhilarating outdoor walk on the roof where you venture across the glass-floored viewing platform.

- Head to **Sydney Olympic Park** www.sydneyolympicpark. com.au at Homebush and visit the venues where the Olym-pics were held in 2000.

- Step back to convict times at the **Hyde Park Barracks**.

- If you are interested in seeing the birthplace of white Australia, you might like to hire a car and visit **Botany Bay** and **Kurnell**, in the southern suburbs. You may wish to visit the memorial to commemorate the landing of Captain James Cook on 29 April 1770. Plus spend time on the local beaches and walk around the nature reserve.

- Those of you not staying in **Kings Cross** might want to go and see for yourself what all the fuss is about during the day, or visit it at night.
- Punters might like to spend a day at the races or a night at the trots or greyhounds.

Day and weekend trips from Sydney

The **Blue Mountains** are west of Sydney and get their name from the blue haze created by the eucalyptus oil in the air above the gum trees. You can drive up to the mountains or take the scenic rail trip to **Katoomba** and say G'day to the **Three Sisters**. You could ride the **Skyway Cable Car** www.scenicworld.com.au taking you 270m above ravines, waterfalls and Jurassic rain forests in the expansive Jamison Valley. If you prefer to stay on the ground you could take a ride on the scenic railway into ancient rain forest. There is a hop-on hop-off **Blue Mountains Explorer** bus www.explorerbus.com.au allowing you the flexibility to visit lookouts, waterfalls, the Three Sisters, the Scenic Railway and Skyway or spend your time in one of the many craft shops, galleries, coffee shops and restaurants. Or, as the area is a bush walker's paradise, you may like to hike along one of the many tracks.

If you like caves, then you might want to visit the **Jenolan Caves** www.jenolancaves.org.au, which is one of the finest and oldest cave systems in the world. Here you will find 11 caves, pure underground rivers and amazing formations. If you are feeling energetic, it's a 42km walk from Katoomba, or take a tour.

A couple of hours north of Sydney is the **Hunter Valley** region, famous for its wines. You might want to visit some of the wineries and sample a few vintages. **Newcastle** is the major town in this area and is home to the 'Steel Works' which provides much of the employment in the area. There are also some beautiful beaches to visit.

South of Sydney is the oldest national park in Australia and the world's second oldest – the **Royal National Park** www.nationalparks.nsw.gov.au. The park is only 32km from Sydney with its main entry points along the Princes Highway. You can also take a ferry from Cronulla that takes you to **Bundeena** which is in the national park. Here you could enjoy the beach or sit in one of the cafés.

Further south is **Wollongong** 'The Gong', with beautiful beaches and the magnificent Nan Tien Buddhist Temple.

Beyond 'The Gong' is **Kiama** famous for its blowhole. Buy some fish and chips and sit and wait for it to blow, but don't get too close or you might be washed in.

Even further south are the crystal waters of **Jervis Bay**, a popular spot among dolphins and whales. Just north of Batemans Bay (south of Jervis Bay) is **Pebbly Beach**, where the kangaroos occasionally surf.

Cricket enthusiasts might wish to visit **Bowral**, in the Southern Highlands, the childhood home of Sir Donald Bradman, 'The Don', and visit the **Bradman Museum of Cricket** www.bradman.com.au. The Bradman Foundation owns and operates the museum and manages Bradman Oval where the young Don Bradman first learned to play cricket. The Southern Highlands is also where the move 'Babe' was filmed.

Further afield in New South Wales

New South Wales is more than Sydney and its surrounds; there are plenty of other towns to visit. If you have your own car, you can explore places at your leisure, but you can also take the train or a bus.

Countrylink www.countrylink.info trains service some 334

destinations in New South Wales. You could purchase a NSW Discovery Pass for travel on trains throughout the state. Trains leave from Central Station where there is a major Countrylink Travel Centre so you can find out what is available.

Places you might wish to visit include:

Canberra www.visitcanberra.com.au is the nation's capital and is well worth a few days' visit. There is a hop-on hop-off bus you might like to take as the sights are quite a distance apart, or you could hire a bike. Canberra is built for bike riders with many cycle tracks. You could also use the local buses which are run by ACTION www.action.act.gov.au that provide good coverage around Canberra.

Visit the new **Parliament House**, **Old Parliament House**, the **Australian War Memorial** www.awm.gov.au and view the Roll of Honour which lists Australians who have died in war, **the Royal Australian Mint**, the **Botanic Gardens, Questacon** a hands-on science museum and **the Lodge**, home of the Prime Minister. View the art at the **National Gallery** or go to the top of the **Telecom Tower** on Black Mountain for a view over the city, visit the **Australian Institute of Sport** www.ausport.gov.au/ais/ or take a cruise on **Lake Burley Griffin**.

It is only an hour or so to the **Kosciusko National Park** the location of many ski fields. During winter you can ski and in the summer you can bush walk. You could visit the Snowy Mountains Scheme, which is well-known as an engineering feat.

You could visit **Gundagai** and see the dog sitting on his tuckerbox, and maybe learn the words to 'The Road to Gundagai'.

Dubbo offers history in the form of some of Australia's most notorious bushrangers and murderers, and it is also home to the **Western Plains Zoo,** which houses many African animals over the 300 hectares of land as the weather in Dubbo is similar to that of the African savannah lands. The zoo has several breeding programs including one for the black rhino.

Visit **Broken Hill**, a mining town near the South Australian border. Many artists live here and capture the colours of the outback on canvas. Maybe you could stay at **Mario's Palace Hotel** where the 'girls' from stayed. You could also visit the **School of the Air** and the **Royal Flying Doctor Service**.

There is an Australian saying, 'the back of Bourke', meaning the back of nowhere. Maybe you'd like to visit **Bourke**, if only to say you've been there, or to visit the **Gunderbook** Aboriginal art caves.

Suggested routes

The East Coast – Sydney to Cairns

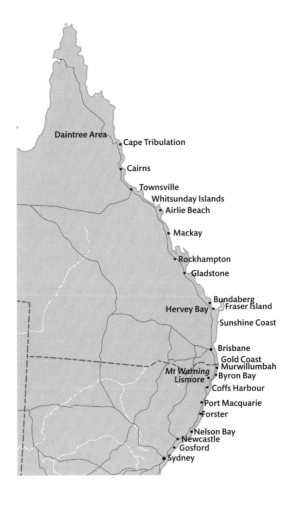

The east coast stretches from Melbourne all the way up to Cape York. Many travellers travel from Sydney to Cairns or Cairns to Sydney. For the sake of this guide we will go Sydney to Cairns. If you are travelling Cairns to Sydney, you'll have to read backwards!

Travelling up (or down) the east coast is a track well worn by travellers. Those with cars will have more opportunity to get off this track and see out-of-the-way things and places. There are many scenic tourist drives, pristine beaches, rainforests and historic sites, and if something catches your eye you can take off and have a look.

Leaving Sydney, you will travel north along the Pacific Highway. Your first stop could be at **Gosford** on the Central Coast some 80km north of Sydney. There are some beautiful beaches here; it could be a great weekend escape from Sydney. **The Entrance** is a popular weekend escape with its magnificent surrounding waterways where you can spend your days on pristine surf beaches, hire a boat or go fishing on **Tuggerah Lakes**. **Terrigal** is famous for its boutique shopping, upmarket restaurants and its position right on the surf beach.

Newcastle, some 45 minutes away is the second largest city in New South Wales. It is an industrial town and home to the Newcastle Steel Works. There are some beautiful beaches here with historic ocean baths. You could visit the **Hunter Valley**, a major wine producing area, and taste a few varieties, not too far away.

From Newcastle you could head to **Nelson Bay** and **Port Stephens** where there are more beautiful pristine beaches and waterways to enjoy.

Port Stephens is off the main highway but this huge port houses many bays and beaches. If you have your own transport, you could travel from Nelson Bay at the south end of the port around to the Great Lakes at the north. There you will find the Myall Lakes National Park where you might see kangaroos and koalas in their natural habitat.

Forster is another place Sydney-siders go for a weekend. Some 312km north of Sydney, this area draws large numbers of visitors to experience dolphin cruises, sailboarding, fishing, scuba diving as well as beautiful beaches.

Port Macquarie is another place to lie on a beach and relax while **Bellingen** is a small town and a good base to explore the nearby Dorrigo National Park. Bellingen has many arts and crafts shops and cafés. **Coffs Harbour** is home to the Big Banana which you might want to pose in front of to have your photo taken. Come on, be a tourist!

Heading on up the coast are the towns of **Grafton** and **Yamba**, at the mouth of the Clarence River, which has become one of the hippest towns on the coast. Check out all the beaches, restaurants, cafés and day spas. For the nature lovers don't miss out on the World Heritage-listed coastal rainforest at the Iluka Nature Reserve.

About 10 hours north of Sydney you will encounter **Lismore** and the surrounding area, a hidden jewel between the rainforest and the sea. This area is also known as the Rainbow Region as it contains nearly one third of NSW's forest reserve, where you can explore heritage-listed rainforests and national parks. Many stop at **Nimbin**, hippy capital of Australia.

The coast road from **Ballina** to **Byron Bay** is spectacular. At Byron, as it's affectionately called, you could do the Cape Byron walk, which will take you the lighthouse where you could see dolphins and whales. Also take in the fact that you are standing on the most eastern point of Australia. Another photo opportunity.

You might want to spend a few days in Byron lazing on the beach, learning to surf or relaxing in one of the cafés. The place is very laid back and alternative and is home to hippies who have chosen to leave the rat race. There is a lot of local produce to try and buy.

From Byron you may like to stop at **Murwillumbah** which is identified as being in the top ten of the most desirable places to live in Australia. This is based on a number of things including its natural beauty and its location in the centre of the Tweed Valley.

Mount Warning dominates the skyline behind Murwillumbah. Here is where the first rays of sunlight touch Australia each day. Mount Warning is a World Heritage-listed National Park of some 2210ha. Those energetic enough may wish to climb to the top.

Thirty minutes north is the **Gold Coast** which isn't everyone's cup of tea. The strip running for 42km from Tweed Heads up to Southport covers some beautiful beaches but it is also very commercial with many high-rise apartments. If ever you wanted to splurge and stay away from a hostel, this is a place to do it because there is so much accommodation catering for every budget.

The Gold Coast is home to a number of theme parks including MovieWorld, Sea World, Wet'n'Wild, Dreamworld and White Water World. You might want to try your luck at Jupiter's Casino or you may prefer to see if you can pick up some casual work.

The Gold Coast is well serviced Surfside www.surfside.com.au which provides a good bus network and runs the length of the Gold Coast with stops every 300 metres.

There are many car rental companies on the Gold Coast that rent vehicles for a day. Maybe visit **Tamborine Mountain** in the Hinterland to walk through the rainforest and possibly see platypus in the creeks. You could also explore the Tweed Valley and buy some fresh pineapple.

You could take a cruise to **North** or **South Stradbroke Islands** for the day.

The New England Highway to Brisbane

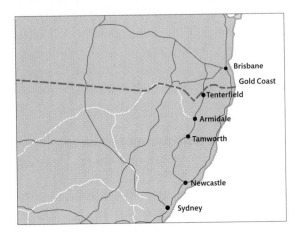

For those not wanting to spend all their time on a beach, take the New England Highway from Newcastle and travel via **Tamworth**, home of Australian country music and see the giant Golden Guitar. If you love your country music you will love the museums and memorabilia. If in town during January you can't miss the country music festival.

There are various small towns to visit along the New England Highway but one to stop at is **Armidale**, high on the Northern Tablelands. Armidale is situated half way between Sydney and Brisbane and is only two hours from the coast. The town has a rich heritage which can be discovered if you take the city's Heritage Trail. It is also on the doorstep of World Heritage-listed reserve, including Oxley Wild Rivers National Park where you might see an acrobatic brush-tailed rock wallaby.

Keep following the road to **Tenterfield**, birthplace of Peter Allen, and pop in to the saddler's shop on the High Street. Tenterfield sits astride the Great Dividing Range and offers magnificent rugged scenery with large national parks and heritage trails.

If interested in fossicking for gemstones then **Inverell** is the place to stop. If fossicking isn't your thing then visit the nearby Copeton and Pindari Dams for some water recreational activities or continue on your way to Brisbane.

Sightseeing Brisbane

Brisbane is the third largest city in Australia and is the capital of Queensland. You may want to spend a few days here seeing the sights of this city. If you are looking for accommodation, enquire at the Roma Street Transit Centre where there is an accommodation desk.

You might wish to take the hop-on hop-off **City Sights** tour to hear some history of Brisbane, and see the major sights including the Cultural Centre at Southbank where Expo 88 was staged. Or take a cruise along the Brisbane River and experience the city from the water.

You may wish to go to **Mt Coot-tha** for a panoramic view over the city.

Plane fanciers might wish to visit the **Southern Cross**, Charles Kingsford-Smith's plane, at Brisbane Airport.

Rum fanciers may wish to tour the **Beenleigh Rum Distillery** to see how the rum is made and maybe purchase some.

Dolphin lovers could visit **Tangalooma** on Moreton Bay Island and feed the dolphins that visit nightly.

Take a cruise to **Stradbroke Island** if you haven't already done so from the Gold Coast.

For an outback Aussie experience you may wish to see the sheep shearing at the **Australian Woolshed**.

Take a walk through the Queen Street Mall, the heart of the city, and shop 'till you drop or relax with a coffee.

Try your luck at **Conrad Treasury Casino** or maybe find a job there.

Beer enthusiasts may wish to tour the **XXXX Brewery** to see how the beer is made and maybe purchase some.

Leaving Brisbane, those with cars may wish to take a scenic drive through pineapple country and have a photo stop at the Big Pineapple on their way via the now extinct volcanoes of the Glasshouse Mountains. Or travel along the beautiful beaches of the Sunshine Coast that is less commercial than the Gold Coast. At the northern end of the Sunshine Coast is subtropical **Noosa Heads**, the Riviera of the Sunshine Coast and a popular spot to stop. You can lie on a beach, try some water sports or walk through Noosa National Park taking in the native flora and fauna.

Australia Zoo www.australiazoo.com.au, home of the Crocodile Hunter, Steve Irwin is about an hour away from the Sunshine Coast. Set on over sixty acres, Australia Zoo offers spacious and artistic enclosures for the many animals it houses. You can see big cats, elephants, koalas and of course, crocodiles.

Next stop could be **Fraser Island**, the largest sand island in the world with a 123km stretch of sand. It is a World Heritage-listed area and is a nature lover's paradise. Four-wheel drives are the only vehicles allowed on the island. They can be easily rented if you want to explore the island yourself, or you could take one of the available tours. These include day tours for about A$100 or camping tours of 2-3 days duration for A$180 plus, and are the best way to experience the island. The longer the stay, the better.

Fraser Island protects **Hervey Bay**, resulting in calm waters. Most people come here to lie on a beach or catch a boat from Urangan Harbour to go whale watching in the bay.

The whale watching season is from July to October. There are many boats able to take you out to Platypus Bay near the tip of Fraser Island where the whales like to put on displays of breaching and tail and fin slapping. Hopefully they might be so interested in the boat they will come up for a closer look.

Half day and full day tours are offered on various sized boats.

As it can be rough out there, those who get sea-sick easily but still want to go, might be better off on a half day tour. Hopefully it will be calm but you can't predict the weather. Don't forget to wear sunscreen, sunglasses, a hat and maybe take a jumper to keep out the wind. Don't forget the camera.

If you didn't organise a trip out to Fraser Island earlier, one can be arranged from Hervey Bay.

Bundaberg could be your next port of call. This is sugarcane country and home of Bundaberg Rum (Bundy Rum) so you might wish to visit the Bundaberg Rum Distillery. Plenty of year-round agricultural work is offered here for those needing to top up their funds. Ask at the hostels about what work is available.

Lady Musgrave and **Lady Elliot Islands** are accessed from Bundaberg and are good places to swim, fish and dive or just relax.

Gladstone is another stop you could make if you want to spend some time **on Lady Musgrave** or **Heron Islands**.

Rockhampton is the beef capital of Australia. You might wish to visit the Capricorn Caverns with 16 caverns to explore, or the crocodile farm. You could also head out to **Yeppoon**, the step-off point for those wishing to visit **Great Keppel Island**. This is also where the **Great Barrier Reef** begins.

It is a long drive to **Mackay**, the stop-off point for **Lindeman** and **Brampton Islands**. Or you could keep on going to **Airlie Beach,** the gateway to the **Whitsunday Islands**. There are more than 70 islands in this group although only **Lindeman, Daydream, North Molle, South Molle, Hayman, Hook, Long** and **Hamilton Islands** have resorts. Each resort offers an array of accommodation from budget to five star.

The resorts offer standby rates if you feel like experiencing a little luxury. Stays can only be booked a couple of days in advance. Ask at one of the many tourist shops along the main strip at Airlie Beach.

Relaxing here for a few days is well worth your while. You might wish to learn to dive or take a sailing trip around the islands.

There are many boats cruising the islands, from small party boats to large, more luxurious and quieter boats. Most vessels will drop anchor for you to swim and snorkel. Some may even have barbecues on a deserted beach.

Most hostels promote the smaller party boats. If that's what you're after then go for it, if not try and spend a little extra to get what you want. Prices range from around A$300 onwards for two or three days of cruising. Where you go depends on the weather.

Those looking for work might obtain a hospitality position at one of the resorts. See our 'Resort Work' section in the A-Z of Jobs.

On to **Townsville** – the third largest city in Queensland. This is the step-off point for those going to **Magnetic Island**. This island is often referred to as the koala capital of Australia as there are thousands of koalas roaming the island. It is also the sunniest spot on the coast with an average of 320 fine days a year.

Day trips to the reef are popular. So is learning to dive. Once you learn you might wish to try Australia's best dive and the sixth best in the world (although some divers will dispute this fact), the **Yongala Wreck**.

Townsville is home to an army base and James Cook University, and is the financial capital of North Queensland. You may wish to try your luck at the Jupiters Townsville Casino or maybe apply for a position.

You might like to walk through the aquarium or go to the top of Castle Hill for a panoramic view of the city and the islands beyond.

Many travellers stop at **Cardwell**, the starting point for trips to **Hinchinbrook Island**, the world's largest island national park.

When it's raining in **Cairns**, many people head for **Mission Beach**, a good place to lie on the sand, or catch the boat to **Dunk Island** where you might see the Ulysses butterfly.

Before reaching Cairns those with a car might wish to visit the **Boulder National Park**. You could walk the rainforest circuit and see the boulders. Be careful when you're walking as there have have been a number of deaths along this path from people slipping on the boulders and drowning in the water.

Cairns is where the rainforest meets the reef. Like the Gold Coast, there is plenty of accommodation to suit all budgets, so if you want that something extra a hostel can't give you, you may wish to upgrade.

In Cairns, walk the esplanade, go shopping or take a sail in Cairns harbour and Everglades to spot estuarine crocodiles, or visit a crocodile farm. Maybe you'd like to go game fishing or take the **Cairns Explorer** hop-on hop-off bus.

You could take a tour with a local Aborigine to learn about the culture of the Aborigines in this area. You might want to try bungee jumping.

Cairns is also a popular place to learn to dive. You'll need five days which covers two days of theory, a day in the pool and two days of diving. You will need to pass a medical to Australian Standard 4005.1 to dive. People with asthma and sinus problems might be excluded from diving as the pressure from being under-water can exacerbate these problems. Don't be too worried if you find your mask has blood in it, as it's quite common for new divers to experience nose bleeds on their first dive due to the water pressure.

Budget around A$600 for a course, which covers meals, accommodation on the boat and the use of equipment. Once you've learned, or if you are already an experienced diver, you may wish to undertake other dives along the Great Barrier Reef including a popular spot, the **Cod Hole**.

Twenty six kilometres off the coast of Cairns is the tiny coral cay of **Green Island.** The island is a national park and offers very good snorkling. For this reason and the fact that the accommodation on the island is limited and expensive, the island makes for a great day trip. Trips can be organised from Cairns.

Cairns, like the Gold Coast, has many local car rental operators. You could drive up the mountains to **Kuranda,** a village in the rainforest taking in the Crater Lakes, the Barron Falls and the Curtain Fig Tree. Or take the scenic railway winding its way up the mountains offering some wonderful views. You could also take the Skyrail Cableway to Kuranda.

You could leave the tropical far north and head in to the **Gulf Savannah** for a trip to the **Undarra Lava Caves** www.undarra. com.au, which are part of the longest lava flow from a single volcanic crater in the world and stretch for some 16km. On the way you could have a drink at the highest pub in Queensland, in the town of **Tully**. Take note of the signs advising of various battalions which were stationed in the area during WWII.

From Cairns many tours can be undertaken, like a one or two-day tour to **Cape Tribulation**, taking in the magnificent World Heritage-listed **Daintree Rainforest**. Spend your time wondering through the rainforest or relaxing on a pristine beach

Across the top – Townsville to Three Ways

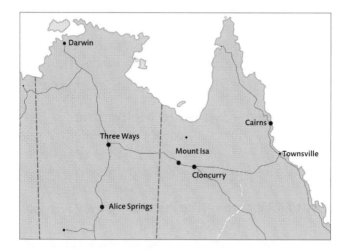

To or from the outback (Townsville to Three Ways) is a long way. In fact it is about 2000km, or a good 25 hours on a bus along the Flinders and Barkly Highways.

Three Ways is so named because there are only three ways to go to from Three Ways, to Townsville, to Darwin or to Alice Springs.

Many who drive or take the bus trip between Townsville and Three Ways stop at **Mt Isa**, which is roughly half way. Mt Isa has the largest silver mine in Australia. The city itself is the administrative, commercial and industrial centre for Queensland's vast north-western region and has some 25 000 people living here. Lake Moondarra, an artificial lake 19km north of the city, provides both drinking water and the opportunity to enjoy water sports.

You might want to stop in **Cloncurry** (before or after Mt Isa, depending on which way you are going) where the Royal Flying

Doctor Service was established in 1928. The town itself was founded in 1867 by Ernest Henry and it is noted for having the hottest recorded temperature in Australian history in 1889 of 53.9°C or 127.5°F.

If you don't want to drive or bus this distance, you could always fly from Townsville or Cairns to Darwin or Alice Springs – a three or four hour flight.

The East Coast – Sydney to Melbourne

There are various highways leading out of Sydney to take you south. These include the Princes Highway and the Hume Highway.

Sydney to Melbourne – The Princes Highway

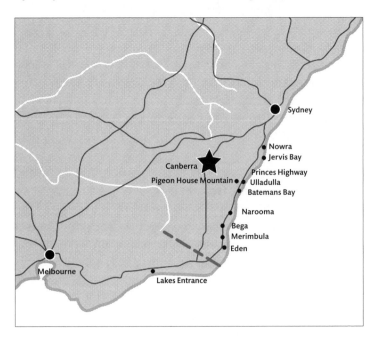

Heading south from Sydney you will pass through many of Sydney's Southern Suburbs. You could turn off the highway and explore the Royal National Park or head over Mt Ousley into the Illawarra Region with its famous bays and beaches.

Nowra is the first major town about 2 hours south of Sydney. It is the financial hub of the South Coast and is home to a number of naval bases including HMAS Albatross. At the base you could visit the impressive plane museum.

Jervis Bay only 2.5 hours from Sydney has some magnificent national parks, charming small towns, hidden creeks and inlets and loads of natural, unspoilt secluded bays with crystal clear blue water and white sandy beaches. **Huskisson** is a very popular spot where you might want to try a spot of lunch at the Husky Pub, visit the Lady Denman www.ladydenman.asn.au a decommissioned ferry or take a dolphin watch cruise www.dolphinwatch.com.au.

Jervis Bay is also home to a number of naval bases. This is because when Canberra was chosen as the national capital of Australia, written into its constitution was a clause that it must be protected by land, air and sea. Jervis Bay was therefore chosen for naval bases to protect the capital by sea.

Further down the South Coast you will pass through towns including **Ulladulla** with its miles of amazing beaches, bays and lakes set against the backdrop of Budawang Mountain Range. Visit the picturesque harbour, home of the local fishing fleet and maybe purchase some fresh seafood or enjoy it in one of the local seafood restaurants.

West of Ulladulla is the impressive landmark of **Pigeon House Mountain** situated in the Morton National Park. This mountain was one of the sights seen and noted by Captain James Cook as he sailed the east coast of Australia. The Aboriginal name for the mountain is 'Dithol', meaning woman's breast for obvious reasons. Today, this mountain forms part of an extremely popular bushwalk. Pigeon House rises steeply to 720m above sea level and you can climb safely to the summit. It is quite a strenuous trip, but you will be rewarded with a spectacular 360 degree vista that shows you the beaches and the Pacific Ocean to the east and the magnificent Budawang Mountains to the west.

Batemans Bay sits on the mouth of the Clyde River and is an inspiring sight as you approach. Batemans Bay is one of the largest towns on the coast but retains a small-town feel. It has beautiful lakes and waterways and some great bushwalks. The fishing is pretty good too. During your visit to Batemans Bay you may wish to take a 10km drive to the pretty town of **Nelligen** where you will find a quiet village and don't forget a visit to the Holmes Lookout for a magnificent view over the town.

Narooma is the next picturesque town on the south coast that you will encounter. It is a favourite holiday spot for many Australians and provides a great outdoor beach lifestyle. Not far off the coast is Montague Island where many seals and fairy penguins live and is a must for visitors.

Next stop is **Bega,** famous for Bega Cheese. You can visit the cheese factory and see the history of cheesemaking in the Bega Valley. Maybe purchase some cheese direct from the factory. A visit to the lookout as you approach Bega will give you a great view of Bega and its surrounds.

Swimming, surfboarding, scuba diving, reef and deep-sea fishing, dolphin and whale watching (in season), walks along the boardwalk or in the bush and fresh seafood are just some of the things to enjoy in the seaside town of **Merimbula**. It has a great climate and is about six hours south of Sydney, seven hours east of Melbourne and three hours from Canberra.

Eden is the last major town on the coast before you head west and cross the border into Victoria and travel along the Wilderness Coast. Eden port is situated on the deep harbour of Twofold Bay and is home to one of the largest fishing fleets in NSW so you may wish to take a walk along the wharf. Eden is rich in fishing and whaling history and, if you visit at the right time of the year, you may see some whales. Barring that, visit the Killer Whale Museum.

From Eden you will travel inland through a number of national parks with just small towns with limited accommodation available. Many travellers will make a stop at **Lakes Entrance**, a very popular holiday spot for Victorian families and the biggest fishing port in all of Victoria. As with most waterside towns, there is plenty of water sports on offer. Lakes Entrance is a leisurely 3-4 hours drive away from Melbourne.

Sydney to Melbourne – The Hume Highway

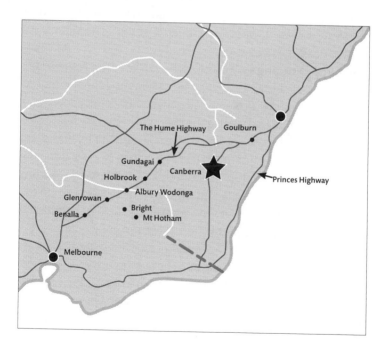

If you don't want to stick to the coast road then head inland along the Hume Highway. You may want to stop at **Mittagong** in the Southern Highlands or other notable towns such as **Bowral** where cricket enthusiasts will find the Donald Bradman Museum.

There are many small towns off the Hume Highway offering accommodation, petrol and local food. One larger town to visit is **Goulburn** where you can see the 'Big Marino', a legacy to the sheep farms in the area.

You may want to leave the Hume Highway and spend a few days in **Canberra**, the nation's capital. From here you can rejoin the Hume Highway and head south again visiting towns such as **Gundagai** to see the famed 'Dog on the Tuckerbox'.

A popular rest spot is **Holbrook**, some 491km south-west of Sydney and 356km north-east of Melbourne. Holbrook is home to HMAS Otway, a decommissioned Oberon class submarine. Visitors of all ages love exploring it.

Albury-Wodonga could be your next stop. The Hume High-way by-passes these two towns that sit either side of the Murray River and the border of New South Wales and Victoria however, a stop in one of the parks along the river would be very relaxing.

From the border you head into bushranger country and a visit to **Glenrowan** is a must to see the last stand of Ned Kelly and the site where he was eventually captured. If not interested in re-living an old gun battle, then turn left off the Hume Highway onto the Great Alpine Road and visit the high country town of **Bright** and the ski resort of **Mt Hotham**.

There are a number of towns to visit off the Hume Highway including **Benalla**, which has the Benalla Museum specialising in the local history, including much of the Ned Kelly story. Maybe visit the statue of Weary Dunlop, an Australian war hero at the Benalla Rose Gardens.

Melbourne is now only a couple of hours away. There are other towns to visit but they are small and are really only a rest stop before Melbourne.

Sightseeing Melbourne

Melbourne www.visitmelbourne.com.au is the capital of Victoria and worth a few days' visit. Melbourne is set around the shores of Port Phillip Bay. The city itself is very easy to get around as it was a planned city and is laid out in a large rectangle grid. Visitors of all ages love exploring it.

There are various ways to see Melbourne. You can walk to many of the sights, take an organised tour, take a hop-on hop-off double decker **City Explorer bus** tour, or catch the free burgundy and gold **City Circle Tram**. There is a good public transport system servicing many areas by tram, bus and train, visit Metlink for details www.metlinkmelbourne.com.au.

Sport enthusiasts might want to tour the **MCG (Melbourne Cricket Ground)** www.mcg.org.au to see the change rooms, the long room and members' areas. You could peruse the cricket and AFL memorabilia at the National Sports Museum and sit in the awesome Great Southern Stand that holds the capacity of 44696 people (40178 seated and 3506 standing). Or experience a game of AFL or cricket at the ground. From the cricket ground you could visit the National Tennis Centre where the Australian Open tennis championships are held every January.

On the way to or from the sporting area, walk through **Fitzroy Gardens** to see the Fairy Tree and Captain Cook's Cottage. You might want to spend a night at the theatre or dine in **Lygon Street**, **Carlton** or **Chinatown**.

You could pick up some bargains at the **Queen Victoria Market** www.qvm.com.au or shop till you drop at Melbourne Central, QV or Swanston Walk.

Speaking of shopping, **Richmond** is one of the Melbourne's oldest suburbs. It is situated near the MCG on the edge of the CBD and is famous for one of the roads that runs through it. **Bridge Road** has an abundance of factory outlets and second hand stores offering top fashion and accessories for the bargain hunter. There are also many eateries on Bridge Road so you can shop till you drop then nourish yourself with a wide variet of foods.

Maybe take in a bird's-eye view of Melbourne from the **Rialto Observation Deck**. Here you can experience spectacular 360 degree views of the city. You may wish to walk through the cultural area of Southgate and retire at the **Crown Casino** for a meal, show, games or spend the night. Maybe a cruise along the Yarra River might be more your scene.

Take a ride on the **Southern Star Observation Wheel** which stands some 120m or around 38 storeys into the air. This ferris wheel is based on the popular London Eye and offers spectacular views over Melbourne and beyond.

Walk through the 19th-century **Old Melbourne Gaol** and see the suit of armour worn by Australia's most famous bushranger, Ned Kelly. Walk in the cell where he was held captive until he was hung from the rafters in the gaol. You can also view the death masks of some gruesome Australian criminals.

See the animals at the **Melbourne Zoo** or take a tram to the **Shrine of Remembrance** and climb the stairs for a view over the city. Visit the **National Gallery**. *Neighbours* fans can go in search of Ramsay Street. There are specialist tours that you can take.

There are many parks and gardens to appreciate, including the **Royal Botanic Gardens**.

Catch a tram to lively **St Kilda** for some seaside dining and take a walk along the beach or on the pier. You might want to spend a day enjoying the rides at **Luna Park**, an amusement park built in 1912 with its wooden roller coaster and other rides, or just enjoy a coffee in one of the cafés or restaurants along busy Fitzroy and Acland Streets. For some lively evening entertainment try the Esplanade Hotel, 'Espy' which has various bands playing and comedy nights.

Williamstown is a historic port to the west of Melbourne. Here you can see historic ships and the much-visited museum 'Scienceworks'. The Williamstown foreshore is packed with historic buildings, nice views and many great alfresco dining spots and boutiques. It is one of Melbourne's oldest suburbs and holds great historical value and is fast becoming one of the trendiest suburbs in Melbourne.

Day/weekend trips from Melbourne

There is plenty to see in Victoria even though it is a small state. The VLine www.vline.com.au (Victoria's country train system) or organised day tours can take you to many places.

A trip to **Phillip Island** to watch the penguin parade is a must. A weekend is preferable on Phillip Island as the penguins come out after dusk and it will be a very late night if you drive back to Melbourne. There are lots of other things to see on Phillip Island including fabulous beach and rocky outcrop scenery with a mutton bird colony at Cape Woolamai. Maybe enjoy the café and restaurant scene in the main town of Cowes, just over the bridge at San Remo. Or visit the Australian Motorcycle Grand Prix track and if here at the right time of year (usually October) watch the actual race.

The **Mornington Peninsula** to the east of Melbourne is a very popular summer holiday destination with popular bay and ocean beaches to enjoy. It is around one and a half hours away from Melbourne. The Peninsula is renowned for some of its local produce including wines and olive oils. **Sorrento** is very popular on weekends and during summer with its café scene and bustling holiday feel. You could catch the ferry over to the Queenscliff on the Bellarine Peninsula on the other side of the mouth of Port Phillip Bay. Maybe visit **Cape Otway** and its lighthouse which the oldest, surviving lighthouse in mainland Australia. The lighthouse www.lightstation.com has been in operation since 1848 and is perched on towering sea cliffs where Bass Strait and the Southern Ocean collide. Take a tour up to the top of the lighthouse or stay overnight in the Lightkeeper's House. Don't forget the wonderful Arthurs Seat Lookout which offers fabulous views of the bay and back to Melbourne.

The **Bellarine Peninsula** marks the western tip of Port Phillip Bay. On the tip of the peninsula is Queenscliff where you can hop onto a ferry over to Sorrento on the Mornington Peninsula. The entrance to Port Phillip Bay is called the 'Rip' and Queenscliff was developed to guide boats into the port. You may be interested in visiting several museums, including Queenscliff Historical Centre, Queenscliff Maritime Museum and the Marine Discovery Centre to learn about the local history.

Geelong is situated on the pretty Corio Bay and has a lovely foreshore, old buildings and a great beach, Eastern Beach. It is also home to the Geelong 'Cats' a Victorian AFL football team. You may wish to spend some time walking around the local shops or sitting in one of the cafés.

Further past Geelong you will find the holiday town of **Torquay** with its great beaches. A number of major surf brands have their head office and surf gear outlets at Torquay where you could find a bargain. Surfers may want to check out **Bells Beach,** not to far from Torquay and catch a wave or two.

You are now not too far away from the Great Ocean Road so you may wish to take a day tour to see the **Twelve Apostles**, spectacular rock formations on the coast, or include them as part of a longer trip along the Great Ocean Road.

You might wish to step back in time to the gold-rush days at **Sovereign Hill** and pan for gold. Or witness the recreation of the battle of the **Eureka Stockade** at **Ballarat**.

You could take a walk in the **Grampians**, cruise on a paddle steamer along the **Murray River** or head to bushranger country in **Glenrowan**.

Maybe visit **Hanging Rock** for a picnic and a climb to the top of the rock, which offers great views of the area. Or go to **Daylesford**, known as a popular spa town for some relaxation.

A popular weekend spot is the **Dandenong Ranges** east of Melbourne. You may wish to wind your way through the ranges visiting small towns such as **Olinda** and visit the local craft shops and cafés. Head to the **SkyHigh Mount Dandenong Observatory** on Mount Dandenong which stands at 633 metres high for a birds-eye view over the area. On a clear day you can see Port Phillip Bay and Melbourne city. You may wish to catch **Puffing Billy,** a steam train that winds its way through beautiful landscape between Belgrave and Gembrook.

Tasmania

Tasmania is the one and only island state of Australia and is a compact and great destination if you want to see plenty of highlights in a short space of time. To get there you can either take a flight or an overnight cruise from Melbourne to Devonport across Bass Strait on the luxurious overnight ferry, the *Spirit of Tasmania* www.spiritoftasmania.com.au.

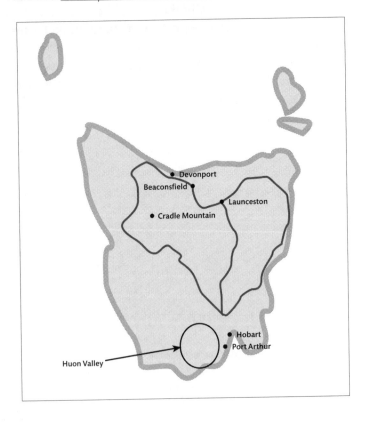

Hobart, the capital of Tasmania, was settled in 1804 by Lieutenant Governor Collins. It is on the Derwent River with Mount Wellington hovering over it. Hobart's European beginnings are evident everywhere with the style of some buildings and they are now mixed with a modern metropolis. You may wish to take a harbour cruise past square-rigged yachts or drive to the summit of Mount Wellington and enjoy the view over the city and beyond. Or head down to Salamanca Place where you can sit in 19th-century waterfront warehouses dating back to the 1830s which have been converted to cafés, restaurants and galleries. If there on a Saturday you are in luck as there are markets here on this day.

Try your luck at Hobart's **Wrest Point Casino**, the first casino in Australia, or maybe seek a position there.

If in Hobart after Boxing Day you may see some of fleet arriving in the harbour who are contesting the Sydney to Hobart Yacht Race which leaves Sydney on Boxing Day.

On arrival, you could purchase a 7, 14 or 30-day bus pass and tour around the island yourself, take an organised tour, or hire a car. Visit the coastal features of the **Tasman Arch** and **Devil's Kitchen** before reaching the historic penal settlement at **Port Arthur**, which gives you an insight into the life the convicts endured as well as the soldiers, civilians and their families. The Port Arthur Historic Site is Australia's most intact convict site. Set within 40 hectares are over 30 buildings, ruins and restored period homes. It is worth spending a couple of days here and paying a small additional fee to cruise to the Isle of the Dead.

Visit the **Huon Valley**, see the Apple Museum and sample some apple butter spread. Or you may wish to get work here picking apples between November and May.

See the alpine scenery at **Cradle Mountain** that is part of the World Heritage-listed Wilderness area. You might spot a Tasmanian Devil. Experience the **Franklin-Gordon Wild Rivers**

National Park and cruise the **Gordon River**. Tour the underground power station complex of Gordon Dam. Or maybe go white water rafting on the **Franklin River**, saved from damming by the 'greenies' and also the place where the Wilderness Society first began.

Launceston, two hours north of Hobart was established in 1806 by free settlers. Today you will find elegant Victorian buildings dating from the 1870s and 1880s. Only a 15-minute walk from the city centre is the unique natural wonder of **Cataract Gorge**. For those who enjoy a beer you may wish to visit the **J Boag and Son Brewery**. For those who enjoy wine there are a number of cool climate wines to accompany the fine dining the city has to offer.

About a 30 minute drive north-west from Launceston, along the Tamar Valley Touring Route is **Beaconsfield** a town rich with a gold mining history. The town received notoriety when on Anzac Day 2006 there was a rockfall that tragically killed Larry Knight and trapped two other miners, Todd Russell and Brant Webb for 14 days. You can visit the Beaconsfield Mine and Heritage Centre where you can crawl through a pipe and look into a replica of the crushed cage that the miners were trapped in. You may wish to continue along the Tamar Valley Touring Route visiting one of the many vineyards along the way.

The Great Ocean Road to Adelaide

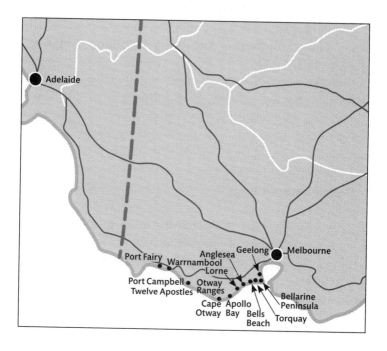

Back in Melbourne, take the **Great Ocean Road** www.greatoceanrd.org.au and experience awe-inspiring scenery as you wind your way around the coast. The Great Ocean Road starts just after **Geelong,** which you might want to visit to take in the sights of this growing city. Then head to **Torquay**, the official start of the Great Ocean Road where you can visit many of the world-famous surf brand factory outlets and onto **Bells Beach** for some surfing. Head along what is called the Surf Coast to visit the coastal towns of **Anglesea**, **Lorne** and **Apollo Bay**, each with their own charm, beaches, café culture and fascinating shops making them great weekend and holiday destinations. The **Otway Ranges** are worth a visit to experience bushwalks in the rainforest flush with tree ferns, waterfalls and sparkling brooks and maybe see koalas living freely in the trees.

The next part of the coastline is spectacular, with the natural wonders of the **Twelve Apostles** and **London Bridge** and many stories of shipwrecks. The Twelve Apostles are recognised around the world. These giant rock stacks, the highest rising to 45 metres, soar out of the Southern Ocean and are a feature of the Port Campbell National Park. The backdrop to the Apostles are dramatic and imposing limestone cliffs that tower up to 70 metres. Though a visit anytime of day provides great views, sunrise and sunset are particularly impressive.

Warrnambool, the only city along the Shipwreck Coast, has a colourful history. It is also a great place to watch for Southern right whales. Then on to **Port Fairy** to enjoy the wharf and a locally caught meal of fish before heading to Adelaide. You might like to visit the **Coorong National Park** on the way to see a beach that stretches 200km or explore the vast wetland ecosystem.

The outback – down/up the middle
– Darwin to Adelaide

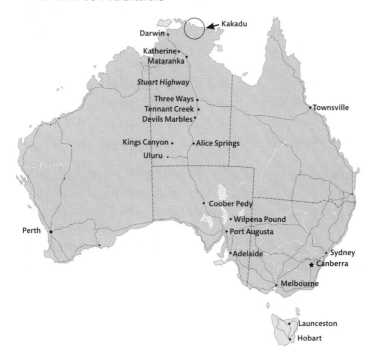

The Stuart Highway runs down through the middle of the country from Darwin in the Northern Territory to Port Augusta in South Australia, and links the major centres and attractions.

If you ever ask a Northern Territorian how long it will take you to get to a place don't be surprised if they reply 'it should take you a six pack'. The joke is, you never worry about actual distance as it doesn't mean much, it's how many beers you can consume along the way that matters. Strict drinking laws have changed this.

There are long distances involved in driving along this route. Many holiday makers hire or relocate campervans (see 'Renting and relocating a car/van in this section) or make use of a Greyhound bus pass. Tours to major sights can be arranged from the larger centres.

From Darwin there are two and three-day tours into **Kakadu**, and from Alice Springs there are two and three-day tours to **Ayers Rock/Uluru**. Some take the Ghan (train) from Darwin or Alice Springs to Adelaide and vice versa. There are longer tours that cover all the major sights and include meals and accommodation. These can be booked in either Darwin or Adelaide.

Sightseeing Darwin

Darwin is a very compact city and easy to get around, although you may wish to take the hop-on hop-off tour which will take you to the major sights of the city. There is also the local bus network offering 14 bus routes around the city, www.nt.gov.au/dtw/public/bustimes/.

Places to visit include the **East Point Military Museum and Reserve** overlooking Darwin harbour, which is where Australia defended its shores from the Japanese during WWII. You may wish to visit **Fanny Bay Gaol** and take a cruise to see the jumping crocodiles. Visit the **Cyclone Tracy exhibit** at the museum and see what Darwin looked like before the cyclone devastated the city in 1974.

Everyone goes to the **Mindil Beach Market** to buy some bargains, or to sit on the beach and watch the sunset. The best view of the tropical sunsets is along the harbour foreshores. The sunsets are renowned for their beauty due to Darwin's latitude and longitude and the smog and smoke produced by controlled burns. You may wish to have a flutter at the Casino where you could apply for a position. Try some barramundi, either fishing for it, or just eating it.

There aren't many places to swim in Darwin due to the stingers in the water, so stay at a place with a pool.

Day trips from Darwin

Litchfield National Park is only a 45 minute drive from Darwin making it a great day trip. It is not as well known as Kakadu because it is smaller but it still offers some spectacular scenery. There are several short hiking trails, stunning gorges and a number of waterfalls including Florence, Tolmer, Tjaynera and Wangi Falls to visit. The falls are fantastic swimming spots where you could cool off, but these are often closed after heavy rain. You can book a day tour into Litchfield National Park from Darwin for around A$120.

If you don't have time to spend a few days in Kakadu then you may wish to take a day trip to see crocodiles in their natural habitat. The murky waters of the **Adelaide River** only 70km away from Darwin is a popular spot to take a cruise and see saltwater crocodiles jump out of the water for food. Tours can be arranged from Darwin or visit www.jumpingcrodile.com.au or www.jumpingcrocodilecruises.com.au.

Into Kakadu

From Darwin, you must experience **Kakadu National Park**, the largest national park in Australia at around 20000 square kilometres and a World Heritage-listed site. An organised tour, from a day to a few days, is a good way to visit Kakadu and can be organised in Darwin. You can visit the park independently but not all the park is accessible by vehicle.

The main town servicing Kakadu is **Jabiru** and here you will find accommodation, a few shops and a visitor centre. The South and East Alligator areas also have accommodation and some services.

Choosing the best time to see Kakadu that suits you is essential. During the Wet season (November-March) the park is teeming with wildflowers and the waterfalls are powerful however, it is harder to get around with some roads being closed.

The Dry season (April-October) is the most popular time to visit the park and also the easiest with roads open.

Highlights to see in the park include the **Mamukala Wetlands** where you will see an abundance of bird life in their natural habitat from the observation platform.

The **Nourlangie Rock Art Site** is exceptional. The best way to see the paintings is to walk the circular 1.5km Nourlangie Art Site Walk. Along the route you will find Namarrgon, the Lightning Man. After viewing the rock art it is worth while to take the short climb to **Gunwarddehwardde Lookout** for sweeping views of the area.

Anther impressive area for rock art is **Ubirr** located in the East Alligator region. It consists of a group of rock outcrops where there is fantastic rock art, some of which are many thousands of years old. The art depicts many creation ancestors as well as animals from the area and include long-necked turtles, fish and wallabies. From the top of Ubirr rock you will have a panoramic view of the floodplains and escarpments which are very impressive at sunset.

For information on Kakadu visit the **Warradjan Aboriginal Cultural Centre** and learn more about the area and its local inhabitants.

Jim Jim Falls is a 200m (660 ft) high waterfall and is an impressive sight. Unfortunately, it stops flowing during the Dry season and the only way to see it at its full glory is by taking a flight over it during the Wet season.

You could swim in freshwater billabongs and see beautiful sunsets. Make sure you adhere to the warnings regarding crocodiles.

Heading down the Stuart Highway

The first major stop south-east of Darwin, some 312km in fact, is **Katherine**, the fourth-largest town in the Northern Territory. It is situated on the Katherine River and offers a range of swimming, fishing and recreational parks. Not too far past Katherine is **Katherine Gorge** in **the Nitmiluk National Park**. There are 13 impressive gorges winding some 12km, with walls as high as 70m. A cruise along the gorge is a must or you could take one of the hiking trails which can be strenuous and last for a few hours to five days.

From Katherine you can take the Victoria Highway to Western Australia.

Next stop some 100km away is **Mataranka** for a swim in the natural springs. Mataranka is the town that was near the site of Elsey Station, the subject of Jeannie Gunn's popular autobiographical novel 'We of the Never-Never'. Some 10km south of the town you will find Elsey Cemetery where you will find the remains of Aeneas James Gunn, 'The Maluka' and other characters mentioned in the book.

There are various places to visit along the Sturt Highway including **Three Ways**, **Daly Waters, Tennant Creek, Barrow Creek** and **Ti Tree**. These settlements are there to service the road and some of them are no more than a pub and a road house.

The **Devil's Marbles** near Tennant Creek are massive granite boulders on either side of the road that have been formed over millions of years. They are about 4m high and 13 to 33m wide. The Aborigines believe that the marbles are rainbow serpent eggs.

Sightseeing Alice Springs

Alice Springs is worth a few days' visit. You can walk around town particularly along **Todd Mall**, in the heart of Alice Springs. Here you will find an abundance of world-class Aboriginal art galleries and numerous artisan cafés plus many intriguing shops tucked away in nooks and crannies. Possibly walk (or catch a lift) to the top of **Anzac Hill,** a memorial to the ANZACs who lost their lives in war, for a 360-degree view over the city and a chance to see the **MacDonnell Ranges** that straddle Alice Springs and run for some 220km. You may wish to visit the MacDonnell Ranges to view its impressive canyons and rugged gorges.

The township of Alice Springs obtained its name from the waterhole. Maybe walk the 4km track to **the Old Telegraph Station**, the location of the original springs. This station marks the site of the first European settlement in Alice Springs. It was used to relay messages between Darwin and Adelaide, and it is the best preserved of the dozen stations along the Overland Telegraph Line.

Maybe have a camel ride at one of the camel farms or go to the camel races. Not feeling energetic? Then take the hop-on hop-off Alice Wanderer. You might wish to take a day trip to explore **Simpson's Gap**, **Standley Chasm,** a very narrow canyon and the **twin ghost gums**.

Ayers Rock/Uluru

The best way to experience **Ayers Rock/Uluru** and its surrounding area is to spend a few days there. Tours can be arranged from Alice Springs that include accommodation (camping is the cheapest), meals and transport. Most tours include watching the monolith change colour at sunset and sunrise and time to climb (although the traditional land owners prefer you don't do this as the rock is sacred). Tour the base by bus or walk the 9km round-trip to see Aboriginal paintings and learn about the Dreamtime and how this area is of vital significance to the Anangu people (the traditional Aboriginal owners). You might want to take a flight over 'The Rock'.

The Rock is rather steep to climb. There is a chain for the initial part and after that it does flatten out, but there are still sections you might need a run-up to get over. Try not to take too much with you as it can get in the way. Take a camera and a water bottle in your bag.

Also visit the **Olgas** which are a group of dome-shaped rock outcrops located some 30km west of Uluru. They are known as Kata Tjuta – the place of many heads. You can stroll through the Valley of the Winds or Olga Gorge and catch glimpses of creatures such as the Thorny Devil (lizard).

Kings Canyon is some 200km along the Lasseter's Highway, a highway off the Stuart Highway. Kings Canyon is dubbed 'Australia's Grand Canyon' with its spectacular gorge and natural features such as the Lost City and the lush palms of the narrow gorge called the Garden of Eden. Kings Canyon offers some superb views and some not-so-difficult walking tracks.

Tours, which include all transport, meals and sights, cost about A$300 for two days and about A$350 for three days. There are standby rates, so look out for the brochures. The longer you spend in the area, the more you see and the longer you have to experience it.

Most of the tours end back at Alice Springs, so where do you go from there? Some catch the **Ghan** to Adelaide, others fly out and most continue on a bus tour or independently.

Coober Pedy in South Australia is usually the next stop, where the homes are built underground because of the heat, which can reach around 50°C. Coober Pedy is the opal capital of Australia and provides around 80 per cent of the world's opals. You can fossick for opals yourself but be careful because there are around one million abandoned mines so for your own safety it is not a good idea to be wondering around on your own.

From here, it's down to **Port Augusta** and on to **Adelaide**. However, 429 kilometres north of Adelaide is the **Flinders Ranges** where you will find the awe-inspiring natural wonder **of Wilpena Pound**. Over millions of years Wilpena Pound has been shaped by weather into a natural amphitheatre 17km long and 7km wide.

From Adelaide many turn left and take the **Great Ocean Road** to **Melbourne**, then finish their circle in Sydney. Or turn right and head across the **Nullarbor** to **Perth**. These are included in 'Across the bottom'.

Across the bottom – Sydney to Perth and vice versa

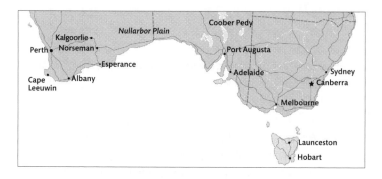

Ways to cross the bottom of Australia include taking a three-day trip aboard the **Indian Express** train, using a bus pass or taking a tour.

There are a number of highways leaving Sydney that will take you to Adelaide. Some options include:

1. Travel along the coast road to Melbourne then take the Great Ocean Road to Adelaide, then cross the Nullarbor.
2. Take the Hume Highway then turn off onto the Sturt Highway to Adelaide. This road travels for much of the way along the banks of the Murray and Murrumbidgee rivers and, consequently, passes through many riverside towns developed when paddle-steamer trade along the river was the only way of marketing the bounties of the riverland soils. The road passes through the Barossa Valley, the Riverland, Sunraysia and the Hay Plains. From Adelaide cross the Nullarbor.
3. Take the Great Western Highway over the Great Dividing Range to Bathurst and visit country towns such as Wagga Wagga before joining the Sturt Highway to Adelaide. Then cross the Nullarbor.

Sightseeing Adelaide

Adelaide is known as the City of Churches. It is easy to walk as the streets are well planned, laid-out over a square-mile grid and are surrounded by parkland. If you don't want to walk, you could take the hop-on hop-off **Adelaide Explorer** tram. There is also a good public transport system servicing the city, visit Adelaide Metro www.adelaidemetro.com.au.

You might want to wander through the museums or along the **Torrens River**. Visit **the Town Hall**, **Victoria Square**, **St Peter's Cathedral** and the **Adelaide Oval** where you could watch a game of cricket. Do some shopping at **Rundle Mall**. Perhaps take a tram to the seaside at **Glenelg** to sit on the beach or see HMS Buffalo.

Take a day trip to the **Barossa Valley** to taste some wines. Don't forget to go to Mengler's Hill Lookout for a view over the valley. Barossa Valley is famous around the world for the wine it produces and here you can visit many wineries, 45 in fact, to see the processes and purchase the end product.

Visit **Hahndorf**, the oldest German settlement in Australia, to browse through the craft shops or eat some German food on the main street.

Visit **Victor Harbour**, once a whaling town and now a popular holiday resort, and take a horse-drawn tram to Granite Island. Maybe see some whales.

Take a break on **Kangaroo Island**, only 16km from the mainland and see the native wildlife and walk among the sea lions at Seal Bay.

The Nullarbor – Adelaide to Perth

From Adelaide to Perth it's a good 35 hours on the bus across the **Nullarbor** and along the Eyre Highway. Much of the highway hugs the coastal cliffs overlooking the **Great Australian Bight**, so get a seat on the left side of the bus (or right side if you are travelling from Perth to Adelaide).

The first town at the end of the highway (almost 2000km away from Adelaide) is **Norseman**, known as the Golden Gate to the Western State. It is named after the horse Norseman who scratched the ground and found a gold nugget.

From Norseman, head north to the twin towns of **Kalgoorlie** and **Boulder** to see Australia's largest gold mine. You might even gain some work there. From here it's a long 8-10 hours' drive (598km) through flat farming country to Perth.

Sightseeing Perth

Perth is the capital of Western Australia. Most people stay in **Northbridge**, a vibrant part of town with many restaurants and within easy walking distance of the commercial side of town.

You may like to take the **Perth Tram Explorer** and hop-on and off at the sights of your choice. There is a good public transport network you can use to get you around town, visit www.transperth.wa.gov.au.

Everyone goes to **Kings Park** with its natural bush setting for panoramic views over the city or you may like to take a cruise on the **Swan River**, the river along which Perth is built.

Spend a day in **Fremantle** situated on the mouth of the Swan River. You can catch the sightseeing tram to tour the highlights. Walk along the waterfront to see the yachts in the harbour, the place where Australia defended the America's Cup in 1987. Visit the **Maritime Museum**, the **Fremantle Prison** and the **Round House**.

Another day take a cruise over to **Rottnest Island** and see the quokkas (small marsupials). You could stay on the island overnight and really appreciate all it has to offer.

If you just want to laze in the sun, there are some beautiful beaches.

Further afield from Perth

There is a lot to see in Western Australia and many of the sights are long distances from Perth.

To get around Western Australia you might wish to find out about Westrail passes, take some day trips by bus, or hire a car.

You might wish to visit **Wave Rock**, about 350km south-east of Perth. The rock has been shaped like a wave by wind and rain and is believed to be about 2700 million years old. A short walk away is **Hippo's Yawn**. It is a long way just to see the rock, so you might consider heading south to **Esperance**, known as the **Bay of Islands**, then follow the road west to **Albany**. There are some beautiful beaches along this coastline and you could do some whale watching.

From Perth you could head south to **Bunbury** where dolphins come into Koombana Bay to swim. Keep heading south along the Caves Road and stop in to see the caves, especially Jewel Caves, which are spectacular. Head to **Margaret River**, once only known for being a chilled out surfie town, this town is now a thriving smorgasbord of fine food, wine and scenery. Continuing south you can go to **Cape Leeuwin** and see where the Great Southern Ocean meets the Indian Ocean.

Over the top – Perth to Darwin

On leaving Perth, about 3.5 hours north, you will encounter the **Pinnacles Desert**. Here, limestone spires rise several metres out of the sand .

Heading north from the Pinnacles you will hit the bustling town of **Geraldton**. You are now some 420 kilometres north of Perth where you will discover beautiful beaches offering many recreational and sporting activities. It is known as a Mecca for windsurfers. Geraldton is a major export centre for a number of industries hailing in the west including mining, agricultural, manufacturing and fishing.

Most are drawn to **Shark Bay Marine Park**, a world heritage listed site because of the enchanting bottle-nosed dolphins at **Monkey Mia**. Everyday, at different times of the day, numbers of dolphins swim into the clear shallows to interact with humans. What an experience!

Continue up towards **Shark Bay** to **Monkey Mia** (which is a good day's drive) to interact with the dolphins. From here, head back to Perth or over the top to Darwin.

Carnarvon, located some 900 kilometres north of Perth is a coastal town with a moderate tropical climate. It is famous for its banana plantations where you might get some work. The coastline is very rugged but offers good fishing, swimming and snorkelling all year round.

Ningaloo Reef stretches some 260 kilometres from near the town of Coral Bay to Exmouth. It is one of the largest fringing reefs in the world and you can reach it by just stepping off the beach. You can spend your time diving with hundreds of tropical fish and the world's biggest fish, the whale shark. You could use **Exmouth** as your base to explore the area as it has lots of accommodation and great seafood including locally caught red emperor, Northwest snapper and mud crabs.

Heading north you will encounter **Karratha** and be some 1,535km north of Perth. This town is known for its iron ore industry, where you may pick up work. It also has a major airport and the largest shopping centre in this region.

Located right on the coast, **Port Hedland** could be your next stop for some more water activities before heading to Broome. **Broome** is famous for **Cable Beach** with 22 kilometres of white sand. There are also red ochre cliffs, bright turquoise waters, pearls and camel rides.

Head inland now through pastoral country and visit the towns of **Fitzroy Crossing, Halls Creek** and **Kununurra**. You might want to make Kununurra your base to experience the natural wonders of the **Purnululu National Park** and **Bungle Bungle Range, Lake Argyle, Ord River** and **Argyle Diamond Mine.**

After exploring this area you head east along the highway to **Katherine**.

Now you know possible things to see and do you will need to work out the best way to travel around.

Travel options

There are various ways to travel Australia including plane, bus pass, coach tour, train, car, motorbike, push bike, yacht or walking.

This section has been designed to show you the options that are available so you can work out the best way to travel – whether that be choosing one option or combining a number of options.

Plane

Flying is the quickest method to get you from point to point but you do miss out on what's between A and B. If you are limited by time or you don't want to spend many hours or even days on a bus or train, then this may be an option for you.

The three major airlines servicing Australia are:

JetStar www.jetstar.com.au which is QANTAS's budget airline offshoot and

QANTAS (Queensland and Northern Territory Air Service) www.qantas.com.au

Virgin Blue www.virginblue.com.au.

There is also **REX Regional Airlines** www.rex.com.au servicing regional Australia and **Tiger Airways** www.tigerairways.com.au a new player in the Australia airline market with limited services.

It is wise to visit each airline's website on a regular basis to take advantage of cheap seat sales on offer. There are also a number of smaller airlines servicing regional areas, which are linked with the above airlines.

If you are an overseas visitor and didn't enquire about Australian air passes before you arrived, there are still several options open to you. For instance, QANTAS offers a 'Boomerang Air Pass' for non-residents and also an 'Aussie AirPass' which is based on seasonality and zones. Visit the QANTAS website for details. REX

Regional Airlines has a 'Backpacker Air Pass' available, so visit their website for details.

If you would like to travel by air but do more than just travel from A to B, you might want to consider Aircruising. Bill Peach (a respected Australian television travel journalist) and Nancy Knudsen created the concept of aircruising in 1983. They offer a number of journeys incorporating plane trips to reach some of Australia's most remote regions and at the same time passengers learn about its history and legends. I have only seen Ayers Rock from the air while flying from Perth to Alice Springs, so I can imagine how spectacular it would be to fly lower and get a perfect 'birds-eye' view of Australia's famed icons. Aircruising Australia includes all your travel costs – accommodation, meals, transfers, transportation, sightseeing excursions, entry fees, porterage and taxes. There are no hidden extras so you know the full cost of your holiday before you leave home. For more details about aircruising contact:

Bill Peach Journeys – Aircruising Australia
www.aircruising.com.au
Unit 20/77 Bourke Road, Alexandria NSW 2015
Tel: 1800 252 053
Email: info@aircruising.com.au

Bus

Traversing Australia by bus is a popular way to travel. The routes and destinations covered are extensive so you can count on being able to visit all the major places you want to see, and more.

The major bus company servicing Australia is **Greyhound Australia** www.greyhound.com.au, which has been operating since 1905. Today its buses service more than 1100 destinations daily on its national route network.

There are three types of passes available for travelers, which can be bought both inside and outside of Australia. These include Oz-Flexi Travel, Oz-Choice Travel and Express Travel.

Oz-Flexi Travel includes kilometre passes where you have up to 12 months to use your chosen kilometres ranging from 500 up to 20 000kms. Or you could purchase a day pass allowing travel for 3, 5, 7, 10, 20 or 30 consecutive days of travel throughout Australia.

Oz-Choice Travel offers explorer passes to 12 of Australia's most popular pre-set travel routes including All Australia, Best of the West, Aussie Coast and Red Centre, Best of the East and Aussie Highlights to name a few.

Express Travel allows you to purchase point-to-point tickets and multi point-to-point tickets.

Visit the Greyhound Australia website for full details of all their available tickets.

There are also smaller bus companies such as:

Kirklands www.kirklands.com.au, which operates in and around northern New South Wales.

Firefly Express www.fireflyexpress.com.au, which operates between Sydney, Melbourne and Adelaide.

Premier Motor Service www.premiermotorservice.com.au, which operates all along the east coast from Cairns to Melbourne. Check out their websites for full details.

TIPS: If you are taking a long bus trip, here are some suggestions to make that trip even better.

- It can get cold on the bus so wear something warm or take a blanket or towel to throw over yourself. Also take a pillow or something to lean on. If you get a window seat you can lean against the window, but I have found that it vibrates so having something to absorb the quivering will help you get some sleep.

- If possible, request a seat near the front of the bus so you don't get the smells from the chemical toilet at the rear. Also, people often slam the door even though they are asked not to. Hopefully you'll have a seat on the left-hand side of the bus so you don't get the headlights from other traffic in your eyes. Take your own snacks and drinks for the bus trip. Stopping at roadhouses can prove costly and the food is mostly fast food.

- Get out and stretch your legs when the bus stops. Just like with flying, the lack of exercise can make your feet swell – buslag! Please refer to the 'Travelling Well' section for other suggestions on surviving long-haul travel.

- People often take night drives to save on accommodation but if you haven't slept properly you will alight tired and lack-lustre and in need of a rest before going into tourist mode. Maybe you can travel during the day, and see the landscape unfold.

Coach tours

If you would like your transport, accommodation and meals provided while being shown the sights by a professional tour guide then a coach tour may be what you need. If the tour impresses you, you may wish to consider working for such a company. You will also find employment/job details on their sites. There are a number of companies offering coach tours within Australia, they include:

AAT Kings Tours www.aatkings.com offers a diverse range of tours that include fully accommodated escorted tours around Australia, coach camping tours, 4WD adventure safaris, short breaks, small group adventures, day tours and charter coaches.

Adventure Tours Australia www.adventuretours.com.au specialises in small group tours for budget travellers, backpackers and private group charters. Tours are available from the outback to the east coast. You can choose from camping and accommodated adventure tours.

Connections www.connections.com.au has a number of tours available to travel Australia. There is Connections Adventures, designed for travellers aged between 18 and 39, and Connections Safaris, specialising in small group nature safaris for travellers of any age.

Contiki www.contiki.com.au specialises in tours for 18-35 year olds to travel Australia. They provide a mix of sightseeing, free time, culture, socialising and adventure. Many young overseas travellers, who are on their own, take a Contiki trip.

Trek Australia www.trekaustralia.com.au offers backpacker travel and adventures including day trips on the Great Barrier Reef, city stays, camping tours throughout Australia plus hostel and hotel tours. A range of 4WD, coach, mini bus and train journeys throughout Australia are included in the packages.

Young at Heart Holidays www.youngatheart.com.au specialises in holidays for the 60 and overs. Don't worry if you are travelling on your own as they cater for individual travellers. Tours have small groups of 12 to 20 people. The pace of holidays is easy with an emphasis on scenic beauty and cultural and heritage-based attractions.

Jo-Jo's (Jump-on Jump-off) and independent tour operators

There are a number of Jo-Jos and independent tour operators operating in specific parts of Australia that provide fun, adventure and usually take you 'off the beaten track'. They can do this because they travel by mini-coach allowing them to manoeuvre better in some terrains. Also, the mini-coach accommodates limited numbers of travellers (about 19-20 people). Some tours are even undertaken in four-wheel drives. You could easily link a number of these tours together as many of them go one-way. Because most of them are Jo-Jos they allow you to jump off in certain places and stay there for a while and then you can jump back on another bus a few days later.

Adventure Tours Australia are a small group tour company offering tours from the outback to the East Coast. Backpackers and budget travellers can choose from camping and accommodated soft adventure tours and package travel deals.

Adventure Tours www.adventuretours.com.au
Sydney: 804 George Street, Sydney Central (near Central Station)
Darwin: Shop 2, Melaleuca on Mitchell, Mitchell St
Adelaide: 115/117 Waymouth St (Just up from YHA Central)
Within Australia Tel: 1300 654 604
Email: reservations@adventuretours.com.au

By far the most popular route for overseas backpackers and travellers is the Sydney to Byron Bay route along the Pacific Highway, which hugs the coast. If you would like to travel from Sydney to Byron Bay, you can now travel through the outback stopping in small towns along the way to experience the 'real outback'. Ando's Outback Tours run a tour leaving Sydney and travelling through Coonabarabran, Glengarry, Lightning Ridge and Bingara before arriving in Byron Bay. For details:

Ando's Outback Tours www.outbacktours.com.au
Email: Ando@outbacktours.com.au

Autopia Tours offers tours from Melbourne throughout Victoria. They also have inter-city tours between Sydney to Melbourne and Melbourne to Adelaide.

Autopia Tours www.autopiatours.com.au
23-25 Gipps St
Collingwood VIC 3066
Tel: (03) 9419 8878, Freecall: 1800 000 507
Email: info@autopiatours.com.au

Downunder Tours conducts tours and charter throughout tropical north Queensland into the areas of Cape Tribulation, the Tablelands, outback mining towns, and south along the east coast.

Downunder Tours www.downundertours.com
26 Redden St
Cairns QLD 4870
Tel: (07) 4035 5566
Email: info@downundertours.com

Easyrider Backpacker Tours specialise in tours for backpackers and independent travellers in Western Australia. Tours range from a 1 day tour to Margaret River to a twelve day tour from Perth to Exmouth, Broome and Darwin.

Easyrider Backpacker Tours www.easyridertours.com.au
224 William St
Northbridge WA 6003

Tel: (08) 9227 0824, or 1300 308 477 (for outside of WA)
Email: tours@easyridertours.com.au

Groovy Grape Getaways specialises in tours for the back-packer market, providing a fun, informative and adventurous tour. Their tours include the Great Ocean Road, the Flinders Ranges, Kangaroo Island, the South Australian outback, and Uluru, Kings Canyon and Alice Springs in the Northern Territory. All their tours are inclusive of meals, accommodation and National Park fees.

Groovy Grape Getaways www.groovygrape.com.au
37-39 Raglan Ave, Edwardstown SA 5039
Freecall: 1800 66 11 77, Tel: (08) 8371 4000
Email: getaways@groovygrape.com.au

Crossing the Nullarbor (the vast distance between Adelaide and Perth) can be a mind-blowing experience. **Nullarbor Traveller** has a number of tours helping you discover the secrets of the Nullarbor including unique wildlife in the Australian bush, wide open plains and beautiful coastline with deserted beaches.

Nullarbor Traveller www.the-traveller.com.au
Coodlie Park, Port Kenny, SA 5671
Tel: 1800 816 858, or (08) 8687 0455
Email: info@thetraveller.net.au

Oz Experience www.ozexperience.com is an Australia-wide adventure travel network that provides a number of 'jump on, jump off' passes. There are a number of passes available including a national pass where you can start anywhere but must travel in the one direction.

One road you should definitely travel along between Melbourne and Adelaide is the Great Ocean Road. **The Wayward Bus** has been undertaking tours along this road in its 16-27 seat mini-coaches since 1990 with its 'Classic Coast' tour. As well as taking you to the 'must see' sections along this road, it takes you off the beaten track. You will visit **Bells Beach** (home of the famous surfing competition), Apollo Bay, see the 12 Apostles, visit Port Fairy and take a walk in the magnificent sand dunes of the Coorong Wilderness area. They also have tours to the red centre.

Wayward Bus www.waywardbus.com.au
119 Waymouth St, Adelaide SA 5000
Tel: +61 (08) 8132 8230
Local call in Australia: 1300 653 510
Email: reservations@waywardbus.com.au

Tasmania is often forgotten on people's travels. To get there you can either take a flight or take the overnight ride on the across Bass Straitfrom Melbourne to Devonport.

You could purchase a 7, 10, 14 or 21-day **Tassie Link Explorer** bus pass available through Tigerline Coaches www.tigerline.com.au and tour around the island yourself or take an organised tour with them or **Under Down Under Tours** www.underdownunder.com.au or the **Bottom Bits Bus** www.bottombitsbus.com or hire a car as distances between towns are relatively short compared to the rest of Australia.

Rail

Train routes in Australia are not as extensive as the bus routes but there are still some wonderful trips to take. There are a number of travel options. You can purchase point-to-point travel i.e. Sydney to Melbourne or you could purchase an **Austrail Pass** which will allow unlimited travel on the economy class of Rail Australia-operated services anywhere in Australia including metropolitan trains. Passes are available for 14 to 30 consecutive days within a six-month period.

Also available is the **East Coast Discovery Passes** (ECDP) which is valid on economy class service for travel from Melbourne to Sydney, Sydney to the Gold Coast/Brisbane and Brisbane to Cairns within a six-month period. East Coast Discovery Passes are available for Queensland, New South Wales and Victoria only but don't include travel on any suburban or inter-urban services.

If you are a backpacker, there is the **Backpacker Pass** available allowing unlimited travel on the XPT and The Xplorer rail services and connecting coach services to more than 360 destinations.

More information on the above mentioned passes can be found at www.railaustralia.com.au.

For train travel within New South Wales visit **Countrylink** www.countrylink.nsw.gov.au, which has a number of train tours including to Canberra and Dubbo's Western Plain Zoo.

For train travel within Queensland visit **Queensland Rail** www.qr.com.au where you will find a number of train tours available including The Inlander – a train from Townsville to Mount Isa. Or try the Savannahlander, which travels between Cairns and Forsayth. Or the Gulflander, which travels into the Gulf country.

For train travel within Victoria visit **Vline** www.vline.com.au, which has a number of train journeys available including trips to the gold-rush city of Ballarat and the popular waterfront area of Geelong.

Great train journeys

Australia also has a number of famous train routes. The most well-known is that of **The Indian Pacific**, which takes three days to travel between Sydney and Perth. The Indian Pacific provides views of two oceans on one of the world's longest and greatest train journeys. After leaving the spectacular Blue Mountains you will travel the world's longest straight stretch of railway track (478 kilometres), see unique landscapes unfold and spot a fascinating array of wildlife, all from the comfort of the lounge or your cabin.

There is also **The Ghan** which runs between Adelaide, Alice Springs and Darwin. Originally The Ghan finished its journey at Alice Springs but in 2004 the track was extended to Darwin.

You can access more information on these great train journeys and booking details through the **Great Southern Railway** website at www.gsr.com.au.

Car or campervan

Flexibility is the name of the game when you travel by car. You can go where you want, when you want and include out-of-the-way places that coach and train travellers will miss.

There are various ways to get your hands on the wheel of a car – all legal, of course! You could rent a car or campervan, relocate a car or campervan, buy your own vehicle or share a lift.

Renting and relocating a car/van

There are national car rental companies renting various types of cars from small cars to mini-vans that you can rent and relocate. This option can work out to be quite expensive if you don't have a full car-load of people to share the cost. Some rental companies give special discounts to those holding YHA membership cards and some of them work in conjunction with the airlines – can you use those accumulated air miles?

One-way rentals can be obtained through the national car companies, as they often need their cars relocated to their home office. So always ask. You may pay a cheaper rate to re-locate a car for them.

Besides the major national companies you will often find local car rental companies where you can rent a car for a day or two.

Travellers often rent or re-locate a campervan, motorhome or 4WD to take around Australia. This is because they are a home away from home because you live in your vehicle as well as travel. For details, including the types of vehicles available and touring itinerary suggestions, contact:

Car companies:

Avis www.avis.com.au Tel: within Australia 13 63 33
Budget www.budget.com.au Tel: within Australia 13 27 27
Europecar www.europecar.com.au Tel: within Australia 1300 13 13 90
Hertz www.hertz.com.au Tel: within Australia 13 30 39
Thrifty www.thrifty.com.au Tel: within Australia 1300 36 72 27

Van companies:

Apollo Motorhomes www.apollocamper.com Tel: 1800 777 779
Backpacker Campervan & Car Rentals
www.backpackercampervans.com Tel: 1800 200 80 801
Britz Campervans, 4WDs and Rental Cars www.britz.com.au
Tel: 1800 200 80 801
GetaboutOz www.getaboutoz.com Tel: 1800 656 899
Kea Campers www.keacampers.com Tel: 1800 252 555
Maui Motorhomes www.maui-rentals.com Tel: 1800 2008 0801
Travellers Auto-Barn www.travellers-autobarn.com.au

Tel: 1800 674 374
Wicked Campers www.wickedcampers.com.au

Buying a car/van is an option many travellers choose. One drawback is the up-front funding required to purchase a vehicle but hey, you will be selling it at the end of your journey anyway, unless you intend folding it up and squeezing it into the little air pocket in your backpack! It is wise if a few of you can pool your resources to buy your car/van.

So how much do you need to buy a car? Of course prices will differ, but budget to spend spend A$5000-$10000. This is really at the top end of the backpacker spending scale. I've seen many an advertisement on hostel notice boards and the asking prices vary greatly; some are as low as A$750.

Even though price is a major concern, what you really need is a guarantee that the vehicle you purchase will complete the travelling you want to do without any hassles. Hassles meaning having to fork out money to have a major part or parts replaced.

When looking at vehicles, you need to consider where your travels will take you and how many people will be going with you. Six-cylinder cars are highly recommended as their engines and cooling systems are bigger and cope better in the hot weather of Far North Queensland and the Northern Territory. However, with high petrol prices, you may be better off with a four cylinder. Station wagons are a good choice as you can sleep in the back. A popular car is the Ford Falcon station wagon. Many travellers purchase a Kombi van because they provide accommodation but they do tend to suffer in the heat as they are air cooled. In a hot area, hot air will be cooling the engine.

Buying a car privately

So you've found the car you want to buy, but before you hand over any money you need to do the following things:

Firstly see a valid **Pink Slip** (this can be called by a different name in each state), which is not more than one month old and states that the car is roadworthy. A **Black Slip** will indicate what is wrong with the car. Even after seeing this you might want to have the car checked over by a mechanic or a motoring organisation. Motoring organisations do require you to be a member. Did you bring your CMC with you? The main question you need answered is: will the car complete the travelling I want to do?

Also contact the **Registry of Encumbered Vehicles** to find out if there is any money owing on the car, like a loan or traffic fines. If there is, and you buy the car, you are liable.

Once these two things are done, check that the person selling the car is the person named on the registration papers. If they are, then purchase the car. I'd be suspicious about someone selling the car for someone who has left the country.

Cars are registered once a year (again, registration laws depend on which state you are in), so when you're buying a car see how much registration is left. When the registration is still valid, the car only needs to have the registration owner changed from old to new. This is done by having the registered owner sign the back of the registration paper which you then take, along with the pink slip, to a motor registry to have your details inserted.

Insurance covering any people hurt in an accident is compulsory and usually included in your registration (it is done this way in New South Wales and is referred to as a **Green Slip**).

Third Party Property insurance to cover any damage to vehicles should be taken out. Some car dealers can arrange this for you.

Each state's laws vary, so it is worthwhile checking with the department of transport of each state about buying and selling a car.

Department of Transport & Works, NT, www.nt.gov.au
DIER – Transport Division, Tas, www.transport.tas.gov.au
RTA, NSW, www.rta.nsw.gov.au
Transport Queensland, www.transport.qld.gov.au
Transport Roads & Traffic, ACT,
www.canberraconnect.act.gov.au
Transport SA, www.transport.sa.gov.au
Transport WA, www.transport.wa.gov.au
VicRoads, Vic, www.vicroads.vic.gov.au

Private sales are advertised on hostel notice boards and in the newspapers. Saturday's papers are particularly good, as is the weekly *Trading Post* available at newsagents or visit them on-line at www.tradingpost.com.au.

Buying through a car dealer

Buying a car through a dealer is an easier process as dealers are responsible for having their cars roadworthy and free of any encumbrances. They can also advise on vehicle registration and insurance.

There are many car dealers where you can purchase a car within Australia however, there are a number of specialist traveller car dealers who specifically buy/sell cars to travellers. They also offer a guaranteed buy-back program. This is where they guarantee to buy the car back from you once you have completed your travels. It is usually around 50% of the purchase which means if you bought a car for A$4000 and drove it around Australia for three months you would receive A$2000 back.

Some specialist traveller car dealers include:
Traveller's Auto Barn offers a range of vehicles for sale with

a guaranteed buyback, and budget-priced rentals with unlimited kilometres and 24-hour roadside assistance included. They are a 'one stop shop' for the backpacker who wishes to drive Australia economically. They have a number of offices around Australia or call them on 1800 674 374.

Traveller's Auto Barn www.travellers-autobarn.com.au
Email: info@travellers-autobarn.com.au
Sydney: 177 William Street, Kings Cross, NSW 2011
Melbourne: 67 Roden Street, North Melbourne VIC,
Tel: (03) 9326 3988
Email: melbourne@travellers-autobarn.com.au
Brisbane: 144 Abbotsford Rd, Bowen Hills, QLD 4006,
Tel: (07) 3252 2638
Cairns: 123-125 Bunda Street, Cairns, QLD 4870,
Tel: (07) 4041 3722
Perth: 365 Newcastle Street, Northbridge WA 6003,
Tel: (08) 9228 9500
Email: perth@travellers-autobarn.com.au
Darwin: 13 Daly Street, Darwin NT 0800, Tel: (08) 8941 7700
Email: darwin@travellers-autobarn.com.au

Travellers Mate www.travellersmate.com.au is another back-packer car sales specialist. You can find them at:
130 Princes Highway,
Arncliffe NSW 2205
Tel: (02) 9556 2113, Email: enquiries@travellersmate.com.au

A place to buy and sell your car is at the **Kings Cross Car Market** www.carmarket.com.au, which is dedicated to international car travellers. Here you can meet, buy/sell cars/campervans from/to travellers. You may only lose about 10-20% on the price you paid for the vehicle. You may even pick up some camping gear. Those who run the market are also available to advise you on registration and insurance. You can also advertise to sell your vehicle on their website.

If purchasing a car, it is wise to join a motoring organisation. Motoring organisations provide services including road-side service if your vehicle breaks down. Each state has its own organisation however membership in one state automatically provides assistance in other states.

New South Wales: **NRMA** www.nrma.com.au
Northern Territory: **AANT** www.aant.com.au
Queensland: **RACQ** www.racq.com.au
South Australia: **RAA** www.raa.net
Tasmania: **RACT** www.ract.com.au
Victoria: **RACV** www.racv.com.au
Western Australia: **RACWA** www.rac.com.au

Sharing a lift is an option. There are people out there who have bought a car but don't have the bodies to fill it, so they advertise for travel companions.

Many lifts are advertised on hostel notice boards and can read something like 'person required to make up fourth on a ramble up east coast. Leaving Sydney on Monday to be in Byron Bay by Friday. Contact ...'. So if you're either looking for or offering a lift, place your ads on the hostel notice boards or try a car pooling agency such as:

Catch A Lift www.catchalift.com
Ecarpool www.ecarpool.com.au
Need A Ride www.needaride.com.au

Cycling

Australia is a relatively cycle-friendly place with many roads now providing cycle lanes. Realistically though, a bike will be all right as transport around the city or for making short trips, however, you will need a lot of time if you are riding a bike around Australia.

If you do get a bike, it is compulsory to wear a helmet. Make sure you take plenty of water, spares and a tool kit. Wear bright-coloured clothes, and have lights and things that sparkle on your bike so you will stand out, particularly at night.

The national cycling body is the **Bicycle Federation of Australia** www.bfa.asn.au

There are also state organisations that can offer information on cycling.

Pedal Power ACT www.pedalpower.org.au
Bicycle NSW www.bicyclensw.org.au
Bicycle NT www.nt.cycling.org.au
Bicycle QLD www.bq.org.au
Bicycle Institute of SA www.bisa.asn.au
Bicycle Tasmania www.biketas.org.au
Bicycle Victoria www.bv.com.au
Bicycle Transportation Alliance WA www.btawa.org.au

Hitching

Since the grisly discovery of seven backpacker bodies in the Belanglo State Forest in the Southern Highlands of New South Wales it is strongly recommended that you do not hitchhike – although people still do.

If you do hitch, have a sign to say where you are going. Be selective with lifts and advise someone (the hostel, a friend) where you are going and your planned arrival time, so if you don't arrive they can alert authorities.

I've heard that if you enquire at the roadhouses where the truckies stop, you may get a lift with a truckie. They don't often stop on the road unless it is flat, as they lose their revs. Consider sharing a lift.

Yacht crewing

This is a possibility for those who want to get off the land and hitch a ride along Australia's coastline. Your best bet is to go to the docks and ask around, enquire in the yacht clubs or leave a notice on the yacht club notice boards. Good times to visit the docks are when there are sailing competitions happening.

You will mostly have to contribute towards food supplies and the running of the boat, but hey, what a way to travel! Hopefully, it will be smooth sailing.

There are not always facilities for yachts to pull into coastal towns, so ask yachting enthusiasts which places are popular.

From Hobart, the boats return up north after the Sydney to Hobart race around the new year. Other coastal destinations where you might pick up a lift are Eden, Nelson Bay, Coffs Harbour, Yamba, Ballina, Brisbane, the Whitsundays and Cairns.

Most boats stay up north for the winter months, then head south for the summer to avoid the cyclone season.

Lifts can be caught to Darwin as many go there for the Darwin to Ambon (located in Indonesia) race in July. During summer a lot of the boats are land-locked because of the cyclones.

In our A-Z of Jobs section, under 'Yacht Crewing', you will find the details of crew agencies that can organise a position on a boat for you.

Companies that can organise your travel

Oz Snow Adventures www.ozsnowadventures.com.au
Oz Travel Bugs www.oztravelbugs.com
STA Travel www.statravel.com.au
Student Flights www.studentflights.com.au
Traveller's Club www.travellersclub.com.au
113 William St
Perth WA 6000

Tel: (08) 9226 0660, Freecall 1800 016 969
Travellers Contact Point www.travellers.com.au
Travellers Contact Point is a specialist travel agency for independent and working holiday travellers.

Adelaide: c/o Cannon St Travel, 110 Franklin St
Tel: (08) 8410 3000
Brisbane: c/o Beaches Travel, 154B Roma St
Tel: (07) 300 87100
Cairns: Cairns Tour Advice and Booking Centre, 53-57 The Esplanade, (part of Calypso Plaza), Tel: (07) 4041 1635
Darwin: c/o Melaleuca on Mitchell, 52 Mitchell St
Tel: (08) 8941 7800
Melbourne: c/o Outdoor Travel, First Floor, 361 Little Bourke St
Tel: (03) 9642 2911
Perth: c/o Travellers Club, 92-94 Barrack St
Tel: (08) 9226 0660
Sydney: 7th Floor, Dymocks Building, 428 George St
Tel: 1300 855 569

Tribal Travel www.tribaltravel.com.au
Tribal Travel specialises in Australian adventure travel, tours and accommodation for students, backpackers and the young at heart.

Cairns: 20-22 Shields St, Tel: (07) 4041 4500
Airlie Beach: Shop 1/402 Shute Harbour Rd, Tel: (07) 4946 7756
Rainbow Beach: 22 Spectrum St, Tel: (07) 5486 8503
Brisbane: 452 George St, Tel: (07) 3236 5805
Brisbane: Shop B, 356 George St, Tel: (07) 3236 1700
Noosa: Shop 4, 28 Sunshine Beach Rd, Tel: (07) 5447 5969
Byron Bay: 1/87 Jonson St, Tel: (02) 6680 9077
Sydney: Shop 5/201 William St, Kings Cross, Tel: (02) 9331 5955
Melbourne: 121A Fitzroy St, St Kilda, Tel: (03) 8598 9822

Wanderers Travel www.wanderers-travel.com
810 George St, Sydney
Tel: Freecall 1800 888 722
East coast specialists for students, backpackers, families and honeymooners.

Travelling alone, safe and well

Travelling alone

It seems the most common reason that people sacrifice their dream of travelling in Australia is that they don't want to go alone. Yes, it is scary, and yes, you may sometimes feel uneasy, especially when you're dining in a restaurant alone. And yes, you will probably feel vulnerable, but don't let these concerns put you off. In fact, I have always found travelling with someone else a hindrance. This is because when I travel with other people I tend to stay close to them, but when I'm on my own I make a more concerted effort to meet other people. Still, be selective and wary of strangers. If you are worried about travelling alone, here are some tips:

- Look approachable. How? Smile at other travellers, let them know you don't mind being distracted from staring out that window or reading that book.
- Don't feel self-conscious about speaking to the person sitting next to you on the plane, train or bus, because you might just make a friend. If you do make a fool of yourself, who cares? You will probably never see them again.
- On arrival in Australia and throughout your travels stay at hostels, as these are full of travellers/students who may be on their own and looking for friends.
- Ask that room mate what they are doing for their next meal. Maybe you could catch a cheap bite together. Or, if you want to see a particular sight: Have you seen it? Do you want to come?
- Join in activities at the hostels, like the weekly barbecue or even watching TV – someone might be watching their favourite show, which could be yours as well. Discuss what's happening during the ad breaks.

- Visit backpacker travel centres to read the papers and notice boards. You'll meet other travellers who have also gone there to read the newspapers or look at the notice boards.
- Book an organised tour that caters to single travellers like Contiki. Try the small tour companies too. Many single travellers take these not only to see the sights but to meet people.
- When you're travelling, follow the popular traveller routes, ie. East Coast.
- If you don't have transport, consider car pools.
- Sometimes employment agencies have get-togethers for their temps; go along and meet other temps.
- If you're asked to join in a social activity on work assignments, take the opportunity.
- If someone has given you the phone number of a friend of a friend of a friend, give them a call. You have nothing to lose.
- Do you know of someone at home who hasn't seen their relatives in years? Offer to pay their family a visit to pass on the latest news. They in turn might pass on tips about finding accommodation or job opportunities. They could even give you a free meal or offer you a bed.
- Join a sporting team or club: cricket, soccer, basketball, netball, rugby league, rugby union, AFL, tennis, sailing, etc.
- Take up an outdoor activity: learn to surf, scuba dive or sail.
- Register for an evening course – you might want to do car maintenance if you're planning on driving around Australia!
- If you don't want to eat alone in restaurants, choose fast food stores where other people eat alone, or go to a food hall in a shopping centre.

So get up and go, even if it is by yourself, because you won't be by yourself for long. And you'll regret it if you don't do it.

Travelling safely

Australia is a relatively safe place to travel, although you should still take precautions to make sure you and your belongings remain safe.

As I mentioned in the 'Packing' section, try not to look like a tourist. Of course you'll want to visit the tourist spots but cameras and maps are dead giveaways. If possible try to keep cameras and maps out of sight until needed. Study the place you are going to before you get there. That way you'll look like you know where you're going and what you're doing.

Even be careful of the way you carry bags. They can easily be slit open without you knowing, particularly if they are carried slung over your back. A suggestion is to wear the bag with the bulk of it in front of you. If it is too uncomfortable to do this, then ask yourself, do I need to carry all these things around? If not, convert to a smaller bag. Girls could wear a small shoulder bag worn with the strap draped diagonally over the body with the purse in front. They'll have to take your whole body to get away with that purse. If you decide to use a money belt, don't expose it when a lot of people are around. Have your funds for the day readily available somewhere else, like a pocket. Bum bags are popular – make sure they are secure and facing forward or maybe have a secret compartment sewn into your clothes to hide your valuables.

Don't ever leave your luggage unattended or out of sight in a public place. Two friends were once asked by another tourist for directions. As they looked at his map he moved them around so they had their backs to their bags, which, of course, was a ploy so an accomplice could steal their bags. The tourist then disappeared very fast.

You should be conscious of where your valuables are at all times. Don't put wallets in your back pockets as they can easily be snatched. If a commotion breaks out around you, hold your valuables close to you and move away as quickly as possible.

It is strongly advised not to leave valuables in hostel rooms. It is sad to say, but sometimes it's other travellers you need to be wary of. Most hostels have a safety deposit box where you can leave things.

When counting your money do it in private. If there isn't any privacy in your hostel, find the loo (toilet) and sit there for a while.

When getting to know your travel companions, don't disclose your financial situation or where you hide your credit card.

In long-term accommodation you might want to put a lock on your bedroom door or on the wardrobe.

  even though Australians like to dress casually, don't be too casual or provocative. Too-short shorts and revealing T-shirts will bring out the primitive instincts in men, sometimes inviting unwanted advances and/or insults. It can also bring out the green-eyed monster in other females who can do nasty things. Other tips:

- At work keep your belongings close to you.
- Don't go into parks and gardens after dark.
- Let someone know your itinerary and keep in contact. If you say you will contact them, do so. Otherwise they might get worried.
- Do not hitchhike.
- Walk in the middle of the footpath, away from the kerb, to avoid drive-by snatchers.
- At ATMs be careful of muggers – be aware of anyone behind you.
- When you're travelling by car, try not to leave your valuables in a place where they can be easily seen.
- If you don't trust the door to your room, put something against it that will make a noise when moved.

Travelling well

Time only will tell if you travel well or not. Hopefully most of us have grown out of travel sickness but for those who suffer there are preparations available, so see your chemist, doctor or health food shop. Prevention is the best method.

If you've never flown before or just feel anxious about it, avoid drinking stimulants such as coffee, tea and alcohol. Drink calming camomile tea or take a non-addictive herbal relaxant such as valerian. If your ears pop during landing and take-off, swallowing helps, along with sucking a lolly (sweet).

Even though it is preferred that you stay in your seat during a flight, get up and move around occasionally. Sitting for long periods of time inhibits circulation. Simple exercises done in your seat will help:

Starting with your feet, rotate your ankles in both directions then stretch and wiggle your toes. Press your knees together and tighten your buttocks. Pull in your stomach. Rotate your wrists. Stretch and shake your fingers out. Rotate your shoulders; raise them up and down then backwards and forwards. Slowly rotate your neck. Have a big stretch. You can do these on long bus and train journeys also, along with any other exercise you invent or discover.

Sleeping, between contortions, is the hardest thing to do on a plane, bus, train or car. You might want to invest in an inflatable pillow to support your neck. Maybe a prescribed sleeping tablet will help you.

Jetlag is every traveller's nightmare. I've read that it is worse if you travel east to west, or was that west to east? Whichever way you go, jetlag seems pretty unavoidable. I was told in a health food shop that studies have shown people with high zinc levels recover more quickly from jetlag. A supplement before, during and after the flight might help. Or else on arrival you can go out, get drunk and blame it on the hangover that you know you'll recover from.

Request only light meals for the flight and drink plenty of water so you don't dehydrate. Spend a little time on the plane pampering yourself by cleaning your teeth, brushing your hair, washing your face and applying liberal amounts of moisturiser. All these things will make you feel fresher.

When you reach your destination try not to sleep until the evening, so you get your body used to the new time. Easier said than done, I know. Go for a walk or to the gym or the beach or pool, if your hotel has them, and get some exercise. Take a long rehydrating bath or shower and apply plenty of moisturiser. You may want to put tea bags on your eyes to reduce any puffiness. Try inverted posture to cure swollen ankles.

Some people take a stop-over on their way to Australia, which is a good idea as it breaks the long flight. If you can't sleep on planes, you might prefer to try a day flight if it's possible. Then you can sleep at night when you get off.

Even the best cast-iron stomachs can react to foreign foods. The only thing to do is eat new things in moderation, drink fizzy drinks (non-alcoholic) if you're feeling queasy and take some antacid such as Quick Eze.

Girls taking oral contraception should watch out for the time difference. There is plenty of sanitary wear available, although in remote areas it is a little scarce and can be quite expensive, so take supplies. Some girls take oral contraceptives continuously to avoid having their periods while travelling. This is something to consider.

A bout of diarrhoea or vomiting only a few hours after taking a pill can mean it has not been absorbed into your system so, once again, take precautions.

Index

Notes

Notes

Notes

Notes

LiveWork&Play Publications

is a publisher of working holiday and gap year guides

Other titles include:

LiveWork&Play

it's more than a way to travel – it's a lifestyle

www.liveworkplay.com